The Healing Properties of Crystals & Stones

By Ashley Leavy

Love & Light

School of Energy Medicine

www.LoveAndLightHealingSchool.com

Dedicated To:

All of the amazing teachers, energy healers, Lightworkers, and positive-minded people that have helped to make my crystal journey possible. I am so GRATEFUL for you!

Much Gratitude

Copyright © 2014 Ashley Leavy
All rights reserved.

Crystal Healing is not meant to replace conventional medicine, but rather to complement and enhance it. Information within this book is metaphysical in nature and is by no means medical. Crystal Healing should only be used with the understanding that it is not an independent therapy, but one that is a part of a holistic healing approach.

Table of Contents

Section	Page #
About the Author	4
Ready for the Journey?	5
Wisdom for the Journey	6
How to Use Crystals Every Day	7
Healing Properties of Crystals & Stones:	
A	8
B	24
C	28
D	40
E	42
F	43
G	49
H	53
I	57
J	58
K	65
L	67
M	69
N	75
O	76
P	81
Q	85
R	106
S	109
T	117
U	124
V	124
W	125
Y	126
Z	126
Properties of Quartz Formations	128
Starting the Journey	153
Tools for the Journey	154
Crystalline Blessings	158
Glossary of Terms	159
Index	165
More About Us	168

About the Author

Ashley Leavy is a crystal healing instructor for the Love & Light School of Energy Medicine, as well as the Founder & Educational Director. Teaching others about crystals is Ashley's passion and her purpose. Ashley's experience is based on almost a decade, and 100+ classes, of professional crystal healing training. Because of her expertise Ashley has been a featured guest on NBC, has been interviewed about crystal healing for over ten radio shows, has had articles published in many more newspapers and magazines (including Naisha Ahsian's Crystal Resonance Magazine), and has been featured as a guest blogger on hundreds of energy healing and wellness blogs. She is also the author of the new book, "Auralite-23: Transformational Amethyst from the Cave of Wonders."

For more information, please visit Ashley online:
Love & Light - www.LoveAndLightHealingSchool.com
Mimosa - www.MimosaSpirit.com

Ready for the Journey?

I'm so excited that you've taken the first step to starting your exciting journey into the world of crystals!

This book has been years in the making, but it has been a labor of love. The properties associated with each stone in this book come from the healing sessions, meditations, self-healing practice, dream messages, and more. I have pulled together all of my crystal knowledge and put it into a handy reference guide to the mineral kingdom.

Because working with crystals is a subjective experience, I encourage you to take the things that resonate with you to heart and leave the rest on the pages here. We will each work with crystals in different ways, and there is no right or wrong answers - there is only your experience.

I encourage you to use this book as a quick reference to how you can work with crystals (but not as crystal healing dogma). :)

"The only journey is the one within."
–Rainer Maria Rilke

Crystal blessings to you always and in all ways!

Wisdom for the Journey

Remember, this is your crystalline journey. It can be anything you want it to be. Let it be magical...let it be exciting...let it be totally and completely about you and your experience with the stones.

Stay present in the moment and be open to the experience. Stay focused and let this book be your guide to the crystal realm.

Let's grab some crystals and start the journey <u>now</u>!

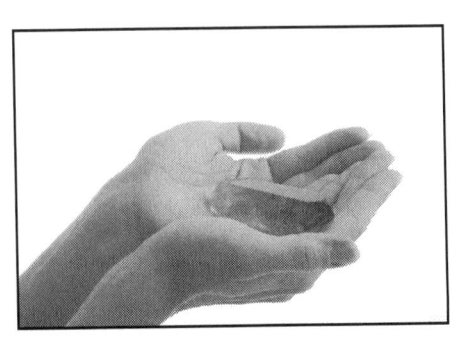

How to Use Crystals Every Day

To utilize crystals in your day to day life, you may choose to carry the stones with you (as a reminder of what you and your husband are creating together, as well as where you are both coming from) in a pocket or small pouch. Alternatively, you may choose to wear one or more of these stones set in jewelry.

You may also place a small bag (or dish/bowl) of the above stones in the area of your home where you spend the most time. Alternatively, you may create a small crystal grid (a geometric arrangement of stones).

Alternatively, you can place any of these stones on their corresponding chakra energy centers (see the descriptions of each stone) for 5-10 minutes (absorbing the balanced, healing energy of the stone into the chakra) one to two times per day.

The Seven Chakra Centers

- Crown
- Third Eye /Brow
- Throat
- Heart
- Solar Plexus
- Sacral
- Root

The Healing Properties of Crystals & Stones

-A-

ACTINOLITE: Use at the 4th Chakra (Heart Chakra) to enhance your connection with nature, to deflect negative energy, and to connect with Angelic beings for guidance and protection.

AGATE, BLUE LACE: Use at the 5th Chakra (Throat Chakra) for encouraging peace and calming, to promote speaking your truth, to enhance crop production and for general plant health in the garden, to encourage joy, to become grounded, to stay centered and balanced in mind, body, and spirit, to relieve symptoms of acid reflux or heartburn, to stimulate will power, to heal problems associated with the nervous system or circulation, to facilitate communication with your totem animals, spirit guides, and angels, for emotional healing, and to block out negative energies associated with stress, and to protect you from electromagnetic frequencies.

AGATE, BOTSWANA APRICOT: (Also known as Apricot Limpopo River Agate) Use at the 2nd Chakra (Sacral Chakra) for emotional balance, to heal disorders of the reproductive organs (especially in women), to ease discomfort caused by the symptoms of menstruation, to help minimize problems associated with pregnancy and child birth, for fertility treatment, to help relieve constipation, to treat discomfort caused by stomach ulcers, to help you to connect to the knowledge of the ancient cultures of the Middle East, to aid in reducing the size of tumorous growths, to instill lust for your partner, to enhance your instinct to be nurturing, to help relieve symptoms stemming from cancer treatment, to aid in treat symptoms of dehydration, and to help treat disorders of the heart.

AGATE, BOTSWANA PINK: (Also known as Pink Limpopo River Agate) Use at the 4th Chakra (Heart Chakra) to help soften a "rough around the edges" personality, to increase optimism, to aid friendships during difficult times, to banish your fears, to enhance your instinct to be nurturing, to overcome self-limiting beliefs, for fertility treatment, and to enhance gentleness.

AGATE, BOTSWANA PURPLE: (Also known as Lavender Botswana Agate, Lavender Limpopo River Agate, Gray Botswana Agate, Gray Limpopo River Agate, or as Purple Limpopo River Agate) Use at the 4th Chakra (Heart Chakra), 6th Chakra (3rd Eye/Brow Chakra) or 7th Chakra (Crown Chakra) to experience things from another point of view, to protect children, to enhance communication and to make your words come from the heart, to enhance your instinct to be nurturing, to protect against childhood illnesses or to speed up recovery from them, to aid you in feeling comfortable in your physical body, to realize your inner gifts, and to reduce anxiety and aid you in living a worry-free life.

AGATE, BRAZILIAN BANDED: Use at the 1st Chakra (Root Chakra) for grounding, for general health and healing, to balance the hemispheres of the brain, to promote present moment awareness, and to bring a feeling of centeredness to the emotional body.

AGATE, DENDRITIC: (Also known as Landscape Agate, Scenic Agate, Dendritic Manganese Agate, or as Manganese Oxide-Included Agate) Use at the 1st Chakra (Root Chakra) or 4th Chakra (Heart Chakra) to encourage a connection with nature, to facilitate communication with tree spirits, for grounding, to stimulate intuitive wisdom, for personal growth, to aid you in branching out into new pursuits, and to connect you with nature spirits.

AGATE, DRAGON'S EYE: Use at the 1st Chakra (Root Chakra) or at the 2nd Chakra (Sacral Chakra) for transformation, to invoke the energy of the fire element, to connect you with the energy and ancient wisdom of the dragon as a totem animal or spirit being, to release blocked emotions, to get in touch with and learn to trust your "gut" or inner knowing, to enhance intuition and clairvoyance, and to facilitate a connection with your spirit guides.

AGATE, FIRE: (Also known as Limonite-Included Agate, Iridescent Agate, Rainbow Agate, or as Goethite-Included Agate) Use at the 1st Chakra (Root Chakra), the 2nd Chakra (Sacral Chakra), or at the 3rd Chakra (Solar Plexus Chakra) to enhance strength and vitality, to provide an opportunity to learn from the fire element, and to reduce fevers.

AGATE, HOLLEY BLUE: (Also known as Holly Blue Agate, Holly Agate, Holley Agate, Holly Blue Chalcedony, Holley Chalcedony, Holly Chalcedony, or as Holley Blue Chalcedony) Use at the 5th Chakra (Throat Chakra), 6th Chakra (3rd Eye/Brow Chakra) or 7th Chakra (Crown Chakra) to facilitate communication with your ancestors or those who have crossed over, to promote cooperation among family groups, to enhance psychic awareness, to facilitate communication with beings from the animal, mineral, and plant realms, to access your higher consciousness, to banish feelings of shame, to promote ascension of the light body, for protection during astral travel, to promote lucid dreaming, and to enhance shamanic journeying or vision quests.

AGATE, LAKE SUPERIOR: (Also known as Lakers) Use at the 1st Chakra (Root Chakra) for physical grounding, to enhance your connection to the physical realm, to connect you with the energy of the water element (the life-giving source), to help you draw what you need from the limitless Universal energy that surrounds you, and to aid you in healing the Earth's bodies of water.

AGATE, LEOPARD SKIN: Use at the 1st Chakra (Root Chakra), the 2nd Chakra (Sacral Chakra), or at the 3rd Chakra (Solar Plexus Chakra) to facilitate communication with animals, to aid in determining your totem animal, to help you to connect with your roots, and to instill courage.

AGATE, MEDICINE BOW: Use at the 1st Chakra (Root Chakra), 3rd Chakra (Solar Plexus Chakra), 6th Chakra (3rd Eye/Brow Chakra), or at the 7th Chakra (Crown Chakra) to aid in shamanic journeying, ritual or ceremony, to connect with totem animals or spirit guides, to gain wisdom and insight from ancestors, and for healing on all levels.

AGATE, MONTANA: Use at the 1st Chakra (Root Chakra) or at the 2nd Chakra (Sacral Chakra) grounding, to bring peace and tranquility to the user, to instill ecological consciousness and to promote caring for the earth.

AGATE, MOSS: (Also known as Chlorite-Included Chalcedony, Chlorite-Included Agate, Horneblende-included Chalcedony, Horneblende-included Agate, Macha Stone, or as Mocha Stone) Use at the 1st Chakra (Root Chakra) or 4th Chakra (Heart Chakra) to facilitate a connection with nature (especially the plant kingdom), to balance the chakras, to promote spiritual growth, for healing of the physical body, to instill confidence, to promote joy, to relieve worries and stress, for shamanic journeying, and to promote intuitive knowledge (especially relating to herbalism).

AGATE, SHIVA'S EYE: Use at the 6th Chakra (3rd Eye/Brow Chakra) to connect you with the energies of Lord Shiva, to aid in enhancing the power of prayer, to deepen meditation, for spiritual ascension, for karmic upliftment (by removing karmic obstacles and clearing karmic debts), to enhance intuition and develop your psychic skills, and for balance and harmony.

AGATE, SOUTH DAKOTA: Use at the 6th Chakra (3rd Eye/Brow Chakra) or at the 7th Chakra (Crown Chakra) to shed new light on a subject of contemplation, to heighten the senses, to connect you with the energy of ancient peoples, for guidance from your ancestors, and to instill an appreciation for the land.

AGATE, TREE: Use at the 1st Chakra (Root Chakra) or at the 4th Chakra (Heart Chakra) to root you to the earth and to aid you in feeling more grounded, to instill a deep appreciation for nature and for all living things, to allow you to channel from the tree spirits, to aid in all types of growth (physical, mental, and spiritual), to encourage exploration (especially for children), and to help clear blockages occurring in the heart chakra.

AGATE, TURRITTELLA: Use at the 1st Chakra (Root Chakra) or at the 2nd Chakra (Sacral Chakra) to enhance creativity, to heal past emotional hurts, to instill a sense of oneness with all beings, to release unwanted energy, and to stay grounded during times of great spiritual shift.

ALEXANDRITE: (Also known as Chameleon Stone or as Diaphanite) Use at the 6th Chakra (3rd Eye/Brow Chakra) to enhance luck, to bring peace and calming when anxious or nervous, to banish jealousy, to balance the body, mind, and spirit, to stabilize the nervous system, and to regulate the glandular system.

AMAZONITE: (Also known as Amazon Stone, Amazonstone, Mother of Emerald, Colorado Jade, Amazon Jade, or as Blue-Green Microcline) Use at the 4th Chakra (Heart Chakra) or at the 5th Chakra (Throat Chakra) for blocking electromagnetic energy, to encourage truthfulness, for balancing the mind, body, and spirit, for soothing and comfort after trauma, to manifest the love of the universe, to facilitate a connection with nature, for balancing the chakras, to overcome fears, to stimulate positive communication, to benefit bone health, and to relax muscles.

AMBER: (Also known as Allingite, Glessum, Glesum, Lyncurium, Lynx Stone, Chryselectrum, Gum Stone, Gumstone, Scoopstone, Pit Amber, Succin, or as Succinite) Use at the 3rd Chakra (Solar Plexus Chakra) to increase radiance, to create joy in your life, to enhance the immune system, for cleansing and purification, to heal the mind, body, and spirit, to banish fears, and to promote peace and calming.

AMBER, HONEY: (Also known as Amber, Butterscotch) Use at the 3rd Chakra (Solar Plexus Chakra) to promote feelings of divine love, to relieve symptoms associated with diabetes, to help you recognize and appreciate all of the sweet things in life, to enhance your motivation and drive toward success, to reduce coughing and relieve the pain of a sore throat, and to encourage a compassionate attitude toward all beings.

AMETHYST: (Also known as Bishops' Stone or as Lavendine) Use at the 6th Chakra (3rd Eye/Brow Chakra) or at the 7th Chakra (Crown Chakra) for protection against negative energies, for blocking electromagnetic frequencies, to enhance motivation, to deepen the experience of meditation, to relieve insomnia, to enhance memory, to promote dreams and their interpretation, to help you to draw healing energy into the body (of the self or of a client), for emotional balance, to aid in receiving and interpreting Divine guidance, to become open to your intuition and psychic abilities, to strengthen the metabolism and immune system, to enhance meditation, to ease headaches, to facilitate a connection with the spirit, To aid in food-addiction and portion-control problems, for protection against electromagnetic pollution, and to heal and cleanse the mind, body, and spirit.

AMETHYST, BRANDBERG: Use at the 6th Chakra (3rd Eye/Brow Chakra) or at the 7th Chakra (Crown Chakra) for finding harmony and balance, amplifying energy, easing stress and as an aid to creating and manifesting. The Brandberg is the highest mountain range in Namibia and produces perhaps the finest energy Amethyst on earth. Healers and "sensitives" have long prized these beautiful and famous crystals, using them for energy work and psychic development of all types. These are transformational, shamanic, metaphysical healing crystals of the highest order. They are considered powerful healing and meditation stones.

AMETHYST, CHEVRON: (Also known as Banded Amethyst or as Amethystine Agate) Use at the 7th Chakra (Crown Chakra) for spiritual ascension, to raise your spiritual energetic vibration, to gain clarity of thought and insight into any situation, to aid in the decision-making process, to heal past-life trauma by moving your spirit above and beyond it, and to reveal hidden layers of a situation in order to better understand everything that is involved.

AMETHYST, CITRINE-HEADED: Use at the 3rd Chakra (Solar Plexus Chakra) or at the 7th Chakra (Crown Chakra) to promote healing and balance of the body, mind, and spirit, to relieve symptoms associated with multiple digestive disorders, to enhance meditation, to encourage feelings of forgiveness, and to direct energy from your place of power (the solar plexus chakra) toward the crown chakra (the body's spiritual center).

AMETHYST, INDIAN: Use at the 6th Chakra (3rd Eye/Brow Chakra) or at the 7th Chakra (Crown Chakra) to facilitate a connection with the Divine; to connect you with your Spirit Guides, Totem Animals, or Guardian Angels; to stimulate intuition (especially of information pertaining to the energy body); to connect you to the ancient wisdom of great, spiritual Masters; and to enhance meditation.

AMETHYST, OAXACAMER: Use at the 7th Chakra (Crown Chakra) to connect your conscious self with your higher self, to raise the energetic vibration of your cells in order to help heal disease and imbalance in the physical body, and to promote clarity of thought inspired by the divine (especially when dealing with the mysteries of the universe), to encourage you to learn and gain wisdom or knowledge that may lead to egolessness and ultimate compassion.

AMETHYST, RED CAPPED: Use at the 1st Chakra (Root Chakra) or at the 7th Chakra (Crown Chakra) to connect the energies of heaven and earth, to keep you grounded during spiritual work, to stimulate the rising of Kundalini energy, to promote the flow of chi or pranic energy throughout the physical body, and for promoting passion (for life or for a significant other).

AMETHYST, THUNDER BAY: Use at the 1st Chakra (Root Chakra) or at the 7th Chakra (Crown Chakra) to keep your spirit grounded and present during times of great energetic shift. The iron content (grounding/low vibrational) combined with the Amethyst (spiritual/high vibrational) makes this the perfect stone to use for treating ascension symptoms, for rebalancing the energy field, and for finding balance between body, mind, and spirit.

AMETHYST, URUGUAYAN: (Also known as Grape Jelly Amethyst) Use at the 7th Chakra (Crown Chakra) to aid you while on their Spiritual path; to facilitate the spiritual ascension process; to cleanse the energy body; to balance and align the chakras (by invoking the Violet Flame of the Ascended Masters); and to bring the healing light of the Violet color ray into the physical body to bring the neurological system into balance.

AMETHYST, VERA CRUZ: Use at the 4th Chakra (Heart Chakra) or at the 7th Chakra (Crown Chakra) for promoting spiritual ascension, to connect you with your higher self, to instill an attitude of compassion and of Lovingkindness, to dissolve the ego consciousness, and to enhance the nurturing aspects of your personality.

AMETRINE: (Also known as Bolivianite, Trystine, Amethyst-Citrine, or as Citrine-Amethyst) Use at the 3rd Chakra (Solar Plexus Chakra), the 6th Chakra (3rd Eye/Brow Chakra), or at the 7th Chakra (Crown Chakra) for enhancing lucidity, to aid in decision-making, for personal strength, to increase knowledge, and to create a connection between you and the Universe. This stone is a combination of Amethyst and Citrine found in the same stone. This combination is due to uneven heating during the crystal's formation. Therefore, it also embodies the properties of both of these stones.

ANATASE: Use at the 3rd Chakra (Solar Plexus Chakra) for removing obstacles on your path to enlightenment, to activate the Merkaba Lightbody, to enhance spiritual wisdom and guidance, for healing tears or holes in the auric field, and to promote spiritual growth.

ANGELITE: (Also known as Blue Anhydrite) Use at the 5th Chakra (Throat Chakra) for manifesting peace and good will toward all beings, for connection and communication with the Angelic realm, to stimulate telepathy, for grounding during meditation, to induce astral travel, and shamanic journeying, to increase awareness, for protection from negative energies, to aid in voicing your inner truth, to promote tranquility, to bring compassion to your life both toward and from other beings, to improve your understanding and comprehension of astrology, for acceptance of your life on the earth plane, to become inspired in spiritual matters, to initiate the channeling state, to balance the thyroid gland, to control body weight, and to remove the heat from sunburned skin.

APACHE TEAR: (Also known as Brown Obsidian or as Apache Tear Drop) Use at the 1st Chakra (Root Chakra) or 2nd Chakra (Sacral Chakra) for instilling joy and banishing sadness, to encourage strong bonds between family and friends, for protection of the physical body as well as the spirit, to instill inner strength during difficult experiences, and to enhance courage.

APATITE, BLUE: (Also known as Moroxite, Blue Pyroguanite, Blue Fluocollophanite, Blue Kietyogite, Blue Estramadurite, or as Blue Agustite) Use at the 5th Chakra (Throat Chakra) to heal problems associated with the thyroid gland, to aid in healthy weight loss and dieting, to promote feelings of peace and tranquility, to open the throat chakra in order to promote more meaningful communication, and to stimulate the power of foresight through precognitive dreams.

APATITE, GOLDEN CAT'S EYE: (Also known as Golden Cat's Eye Pyroguanite, Golden Cat's Eye Kietyogite, Golden Cat's Eye Fluocollophanite, Golden Cat's Eye Estramadurite, or as Golden Cat's Eye Agustite) Use at the 3rd Chakra (Solar Plexus Chakra) or at the 4th Chakra (Heart Chakra) to bring the light of the divine into the heart, to enhance inner strength and will power, to aid in the absorption of nutrients form your food, to facilitate a connection with the earth and with the sun, to aid you in recognizing the importance of the planetary and other astrological influences, and to remove the ego from delicate situations.

APATITE, GREEN: (Also known as Asparagus Stone, Green Pyroguanite, Green Kietyogite, Green Fluocollophanite, Green Estramadurite, Green Agustite, or as Asparagolite) Use at the 4th Chakra (Heart Chakra) for disintegrating negative energy, for physical healing, to open the heart chakra or to keep it open after a traumatic situation or experience, to energize the physical body, to nourish the spirit, for increasing energy and vitality, to aid in the assimilation of vitamins and nutrients (especially calcium and iron), and to balance the body, mind, and spirit.

APOPHYLLITE, COLORLESS: (Also known as Fish-Eye Stone) Use at the 6th Chakra (3rd Eye/Brow Chakra) or 7th Chakra (Crown Chakra) to promote clarity, to facilitate astral travel and lucid dreaming, to assist in dream healing, to enhance Reiki healing practices, for purifying or cleansing your aura or energy environment, to bring spiritual progress, to aid you in changing karmic patterns and to release you from karmic cycles, to open the crown chakra to universal energy and divine wisdom, to help you to realize your perfect nature, and to aid in the ascension process.

APOPHYLLITE, GREEN: (Also known as Fluorapophyllite or as Green Fish-Eye Stone) Use at the 4th Chakra (Heart Chakra) or at the 7th Chakra (Crown Chakra) to facilitate astral travel and lucid dreaming, to assist in dream healing, to enhance Reiki or other energy healing practices, to open your heart and allow you to receive angelic love and protection, for purifying or cleansing your aura or energy environment, to connect you with nature and to the fairy realm (including all of its creatures), to open the crown chakra to universal energy and divine wisdom, to help you to realize your perfect nature, and to aid in the ascension process.

AQUAMARINE: (Also known as Blue Beryl) Use at the 5th Chakra (Throat Chakra) for promoting acceptance, to encourage calm energy and tranquility, to stimulate creativity, to relieve stress and anxiety, to balance your emotions, and to enhance group cooperation and communication.

ARAGONITE, BLUE: (Also known as Blue Iron Bloom) Use at the 5th Chakra (Throat Chakra) to connect with your spirit guides and angels, to connect you with the air element, to cool fiery or angry energies, to bring joy to the user, to instill courage and to act as a shield against negativity, and to reduce stress.

ARAGONITE, BROWN: (Also known as Brown Iron Bloom) Use at the 1st Chakra (Root Chakra) or at the 2nd Chakra (Sacral Chakra) to help you solve problems by multi-tasking and by considering many different options at once, to help you to release the fear of water or of drowning, to aid in transformation (physical, emotional, and spiritual), and to help someone to become well-rounded.

ARAGONITE, COLORLESS: (Also known as Colorless Iron Bloom) Use at the 1st Chakra (Root Chakra) or at the 7th Chakra (Crown Chakra) to promote spiritual clarity, to aid in channeling, to promote deep meditation, to instill a feeling of tranquility and calmness, and to aid in transformation (physical, emotional, spiritual).

ARAGONITE, GOLDEN RAY: (Also known as Golden Ray Iron Bloom) Use at the 3rd Chakra (Solar Plexus Chakra) or at the 7th Chakra (Crown Chakra) to relieve symptoms of Seasonal Affective Disorder (S.A.D.) by bringing the light and warmth of the sun into the body, to bring inner joy that shines forth and affects those around you, to facilitate a connection with the divine, to help you achieve a feeling of oneness with all beings, to promote feelings of gratitude and love, and to help you overcome life's most difficult obstacles.

ASTROPHYLLITE: Use at the 7th Chakra (Crown Chakra) to open the crown chakra to allow universal healing energy to flow in and cleanse the body, mind, and spirit, to heal past life trauma, to encourage you to reach for your goals, as a reminder to be in the present and to live in the moment, and to instill feelings of gratitude for what you have in life.

ATLANTISITE: (Also known as Atlantis Stone, as Stitchitite-Serpentine or as Serpentine-Stitchitite) Use at the 6th Chakra (3rd Eye/Brow Chakra) or at the 7th Chakra (Crown Chakra) to aid in connecting you with the ancient civilizations of Atlantis and Lemuria and to help heal past life trauma stemming from incarnations there, to aid in relieving digestive upset, to enhance your connection with nature and the plant kingdom, to enhance your knowledge and wisdom of how to use herbs and healing plants, and to open the 3rd eye chakra and stimulate your clairvoyant gifts (psychic sight).

AURALITE-23: Use at the 6th Chakra (3rd Eye/Brow Chakra) or at the 7th Chakra (Crown Chakra) to activate higher levels of conscious awareness, to enhance meditation, to energize the Merkaba Energy Body, and for Lightbody Activation.

AVALONITE: (Also known as Blue Druzy Chalcedony) Use at the 5th Chakra (Throat Chakra) to facilitate a connection with your spirit guides, guardian angels, and totem animals,) to help you to resist temptation, for protection, to enhance meditation, to promote general health, to stimulate vitality, to balance the male and female energies in your energy body, to heal wounds of the flesh, to create a portal for connecting with those on the other side, and to give you strength.

AVENTURINE, GREEN: (Also known as Green Quartz, Love Stone, Indian Jade, Green Avanturine, or Green Adventurine) Use at the 4th Chakra (Heart Chakra) for healing the physical body, to increase wealth and prosperity, to protect gardens and homes from electromagnetic pollution, to turn negative energy into positive energy, to encourage compassion, to stimulate will power and confidence, for use during past life regressions and ascensions, for balance of the mind, body, and soul, to stimulate creativity in artistic endeavors, to promote peace and calming, for protection, to aid in problems related to the nervous system, to help prevent heart-related conditions such as heart attack, for spiritual ascension, to enhance inner-strength, to relieve symptoms of allergies, to remove headache and migraine pain, and to diminish acne and other skin problems.

AVENTURINE, WHITE: (Also known as White Quartz, White Avanturine, or White Adventurine) Use at the 7th Chakra (Crown Chakra) for purification of mind, body, and spirit, to instill a high standard of values, morals, and ethics, to cleanse any negativity from the aura and to repair any voids within the energy body, and for spiritual ascension.

AXINITE: Use at the 6th Chakra (3rd Eye/Brow Chakra) for removing entities and attachments from the energy body, for psychic clearing and cleansing, to remove blockages at the 3rd Eye, to enhance intuition and psychic skills, and to encourage you to remove that which is no longer serving you in this lifetime.

AZEZTULITE: Use at the 7th Chakra (Crown Chakra) for spiritual ascension, to enhance meditation and prayer (especially for world peace), to stimulate the merkaba energy body, to aid in the interpretation on sacred geometrical patterns in everyday life, to aid in the creation of energetic vortices, and to bring a feeling of peace and calming to the user.

AZURITE: (Also known as Chessylite, Chessy Copper, Lasur, Blue Malachite, or as Kuanos) Use at the 6th Chakra (3rd Eye/Brow Chakra) to enhance a connection with the Earth, to facilitate the growth of your nurturing qualities, to enhance psychic vision and mystical experience, for protection during astral travel, and to aid in acceptance of your natural intuitive gifts.

-B-

BAMBOO STONE: (Also known as Bamboo Stone Jasper or as Bamboo Jasper) Use at the 1st Chakra (Root Chakra) or at the 4th Chakra (Heart Chakra) to promote personal growth, to connect you with nature, to encourage physical regeneration (to heal flesh wounds, to mend broken bones, or to reverse bone loss from osteoporosis), to instill a zen-like state of mind, and to enhance your meditation practices.

BARITE, BLUE: Use at the 5th Chakra (Throat Chakra) and at the 6th Chakra (3rd Eye/Brow Chakra) to enhance communication with spirit guides, to promote psychic sight and vision, for clarity, and to clear blockages on a Karmic level.

BARITE, BROWN ROSE: (Also known as Brown Barite Desert Rose) Use at the 1st Chakra (Root Chakra/Base Charka), 2nd Chakra (Sacral Chakra), or at the 4th Chakra (Heart Chakra) to promote healing of the heart (physical or emotional), to help your heart blossom into the rose of love, to enhance feelings of sharing and communication (especially between lovers), and for instilling a sense of independence (especially when co-dependence has been a problem).

BARITE, COLORLESS: Use at the 1st Chakra (Root Chakra) or at the 6th Chakra (3rd Eye/Brow Chakra) to allow you to see things more clearly, to provide you with new opportunities, to aid you in keeping your composure during difficult times, and to give you strength (metal or physical).

BARITE, GOLDEN: Use at the 3rd Chakra (Solar Plexus Chakra) or at the 4th Chakra (Heart Chakra) for happiness and joy, to feel connected with Divine energy, to promote a feeling of Oneness, and to clear and dissolve blockages in the Heart Chakra.

BARITE, PEACH: Use at the 2nd Chakra (Sacral Chakra) or at the 4th Chakra (Heart Chakra) to enhance feminine energy, to aid in inner reflection, to promote peace and calming, to stimulate growth in plants, to encourage healthy eating habits, to aid in nutrient absorption form food intake, and to keep you grounded during times of turmoil.

BASALT: Use at the 1st Chakra (Root Chakra) for grounding, to enhance vitality, for motivation (especially when beginning new projects or journeys), and to facilitate journey-work in order to heal trauma in your ancestral line that is continuing to cause present-life conflicts.

BISMUTH: Use at any chakra. Bismuth is a semi-metal. In nature, it is silver-gray and is not found in its crystallized form. Bismuth does not crystallize naturally, because there is usually not enough space for its crystals to form properly. With a little help from humans, it is melted and re-crystallized into a beautiful iridescent rainbow form. Bismuth is excellent for improving concentration and visualization, especially for use during Shamanic journeying. It aids in the shape-shifting practices of the brujo/bruja. It has also been known for its ability to lift your awareness to the celestial realm while maintaining grounding. Bismuth is a stone of transformation, moving things from chaos to order. In addition, Bismuth has been known to promote cooperation in group situations and also in relationships.

BLOODSTONE: (Also known as Heliotrope or as Bloodstone Jasper) (Also known as Heliotrope or Bloodstone Jasper) Use at the 1st Chakra (Root Chakra) or at the 4th Chakra (Heart Chakra) for cleansing the blood, for general healing of the physical body, to transform negative energy into positive energy, to aid in receiving guidance from the inner self, for grounding, for protection, to encourage dreaming, to increase vitality and vigor, to promote feelings of courage and confidence, to facilitate brave actions, to aid in trusting your intuition and acting upon it, to stimulate the immune system, to cleanse and purify the energy body, to ease matters of the heart, to detoxify the physical body, and to aid in the proper blood circulation.

BOJI STONES: Use at the 1st Chakra (Root Chakra) to connect you with a feeling of Universal Oneness, for grounding, for protection, to remove the ego, to facilitate a connection with nature, to instill courage, to reduce stress, to remove pain, and to help treat disorders of the blood.

BORNITE: (Also know as Peacock Ore, as Peacock Rock, or as Chalcopyrite) Use at any chakra for stimulating creativity, to relieve arthritis pain, to balance nutrients in the body, to instill inner-strength, to balance and strengthen the chakras, to encourage happiness and joy, to remove negativity, and to increase vitality.

BRAZILIANITE: Use at the 4th Chakra (Heart Chakra) to bring healing energy into the heart, to aid in facilitating successful shamanic healing, to help you absorb nutrients from your food into the body, to heal afflictions of the skin, and to heal problems caused by fungal or bacterial infections.

BRONZITE: Use at the 1st Chakra (Root Chakra) or 2nd Chakra (Sacral Chakra) to balance masculine and feminine energies, for grounding the astral body during astral travel, for physical healing (especially of the major organ systems), to enhance self-confidence, for inner-reflection, and to promote radiance.

BUDDSTONE: (Also known as African Jade, as Plasma, or as Budstone) Use at the 4th Chakra (Heart Chakra) to balance and align all chakras, to treat disorders of the blood and to regulate circulation or blood pressure, to help in the speedy recovery of unhealthy plants, and to enhance your connection with nature.

BUSTAMITE: Use at the 4th Chakra (Heart Chakra) to enhance the energy of other crystals, to provide a feeling of being nurtured and supported, and to encourage you to find and pursue your true calling in life.

BYTOWNITE: (Also known as Golden Labradorite) Use at the 7th Chakra (Crown Chakra) to instill Divine wisdom, to connect with Angelic guides, to enhance meditation, for safety during astral travel and dream work, and to aid in reliving ascension symptoms.

-C-

CACOXENITE: Use at the 3rd Chakra (Solar Plexus Chakra) or at the 7th Chakra (Crown Chakra) to raise your energetic vibration, to push negativity form your energy field, to enhance the healing qualities of other minerals, for inspiration, to enhance meditation practices, and to shed new light on a situation.

CALCITE, APPLE: Use at the 1st Chakra (Root Chakra) or at the 2nd Chakra (Sacral Chakra) to help you to resist temptation, to promote general health, to stimulate vitality, to balance the male and female energies in your energy body, to allow you to become a clear and perfect channel for divine universal healing energy, and to heal problems of the reproductive organs.

CALCITE, AQUA: (Also known as Lemurian Aquatine Calcite) Use at the 5th Chakra (Throat Chakra) to aid in communicating with higher beings, to facilitate a connection with ancient cultures (especially Atlantis and Lemuria), to connect you with your spirit guides, guardian angels, and spirit guides, to help heal past life trauma, to promote spiritual ascension, and for karmic upliftment.

CALCITE, BLUE: Use at the 5th Chakra (Throat Chakra) to cool the flames of anger, to strengthen the bones, to relieve inflammation and joint pain, as a remedy for cold and flu symptoms, to promote peace and tranquility, to balance the emotions, to encourage truth in communication, and to promote happiness and joy.

CALCITE, COLORLESS: (Also known as Optical Calcite, White Calcite, and Iceland Spar) Use at the 7th Chakra (Crown Chakra) for intensifying visual imagery during meditation, astral travel, dreaming, and shamanic journeying, to heal the eyes, to reveal the veiled meaning in a situation, to relieve headache tension, to cleanse the aura, to cleanse you and your environment of negative energies, to increase vitality, to quicken your spiritual development, to increase awareness, to facilitate intuitive visions and psychic powers, to aid in channeling, to encourage motivation and dispel laziness, to stimulate the memory, to heal damaged tissues in the body, to boost the immune system, and to remove warts and other skin blemishes such as acne. PLEASE NOTE: This stone is only known as Optical Calcite or Iceland Spar when it is held up to images or words and creates a double-refracted image.

CALCITE, COBALTOAN: (Also known as Cobalto Calcite) Use at the 4th Chakra (Heart Chakra) to lift your spirits, for healing the emotional body, to create feelings of safety (especially in places where you feel uneasy), and to promote compassion and empathy.

CALCITE, EMERALD: (Also known as Emerald Green Calcite) Use at the 3rd Chakra (Solar Plexus Chakra) or at the 4th Chakra (Heart Chakra) for instilling a sense of self-love, to heal a broken heart, for grounding, for protection, to shield the aura from outside energies, and to balance the heart chakra.

CALCITE, GOLDEN: (Also known Gold Calcite) Use at the 2nd Chakra (Sacral Chakra) or at the 3rd Chakra (Solar Plexus Chakra) to enhance self-confidence, to let your inner light shine through and be seen by others, to aid in disorders of the digestive system, to increase joy and happiness, to increase prosperity and abundance, to stabilize the emotional body, and to enhance your "attitude of gratitude".

CALCITE, GREEN: Use at the 4th Chakra (Heart Chakra) to enhance vitality, to remove illness or infection, to diminish jealous behaviors, to remove joint pain, to stimulate plant growth, to enhance your connection with nature, and to remove negative thought allowing you to have a more positive outlook.

CALCITE, HONEY: Use at the 2nd Chakra (Sacral Chakra) or at the 3rd Chakra (Solar Plexus Chakra) to bring the energy of the sun into the body, to enhance feelings of warmth and healing while you are ill (especially with flu-like symptoms), to instill joy and happiness, to balance your male and female energies, to aid in shamanic journeying, to enhance meditation and conscious awareness, for increasing the effectiveness of breath-work, to relieve digestive complaints, and to eliminate nausea (especially when associated with pregnancy).

CALCITE, MARIPOSA: Use at the 2nd Chakra (Sacral Chakra) or at the 3rd Chakra (Solar Plexus Chakra) for enhancing creativity, to help you see your own inner beauty, and for bringing happiness and joy into your life (and to help you bring happiness into the lives of others).

CALCITE, ORANGE: Use at the 2nd Chakra (Sacral Chakra) to cleanse and detoxify the physical body, to banish depression, to heal the reproductive system, to cleanse you and your environment of negative energies, to increase vitality, to quicken your spiritual development, to increase awareness, to facilitate intuitive visions and psychic powers, to aid in channeling, to encourage motivation and dispel laziness, to stimulate the memory, to heal damaged tissues in the body, to boost the immune system, and to remove warts & other skin blemishes such as acne.

CALCITE, PINK: (Also known as Mangano Calcite or as Manganoan Calcite) Use at the 2nd Chakra (Sacral Chakra) or at the 4th Chakra (Heart Chakra) to help soften harsh or rough personalities, to remove feelings of bitterness (and to transmute them into feelings of compassion, forgiveness, or understanding), to instill a sense of gratitude (even for the little things that life has to offer us), to help heal afflictions of the skin (including blemishes and rashes), to promote cooperation (especially within large groups), and to help heal childhood trauma (especially when it stems form abuse or neglect).

CALCITE, RAINBOW: Use at any chakra. This is a banded variety of Calcite that contains many varied colors. It holds the combined properties of any color of Calcite that is exhibited in the specific piece. Additionally, it is good for instilling happiness and joy, to promote positive thinking, and to heal negative feelings from emotional trauma.

CALCITE, RED: Use at the 1st Chakra (Root Chakra) to purify the blood, to detoxify the internal organs, to help heal injured muscle tissues, to connect you with the fire element, and to aid the birthing and delivery process.

CALCITE, RED CORAL: Use at the 2nd Chakra (Sacral Chakra) for emotional balance, to heal problems associated with the reproductive organs, to connect you with the water element, and to heal disorders of the blood.

CALCITE, ROOTBEER: Use at the 2nd Chakra (Sacral Chakra) to allow you to communicate with your inner self, to facilitate a playful relationship with your inner child, to balance the emotions, to bring inner joy and happiness, to help relieve intestinal upset, and to remove feelings that may keep you from treating you with the love he or she deserves.

CALCITE, TANGERINE: Use at the 1st Chakra (Root Chakra) or at the 2nd Chakra (Sacral Chakra) for emotional balance, to bring life force energy int the body, to boost the immune system, to aid in recovering from illness and to fight off infection.

CALSILICA, RAINBOW: Use at any Chakra for aligning the spiritual, emotional, physical, and astral bodies and for balancing chakra energy.

CARNELIAN: (Also known as Carnelian Agate or as Sard) Use at the 1st Chakra (Root Chakra), 2nd Chakra (Sacral Chakra), or 4th Chakra (Heart Chakra) for grounding, to increase motivation, to increase vitality, to cleanse other stones, for protection of those who are crossing over, to stimulate success in business endeavors, to aid in overcoming negative thought patterns, to increase sexual energy, to help improve concentration, for peace and calming, to banish negativity, to help heal lower back problems and remove pain, to quicken the healing of bones, to treat sluggish digestion and to increase your digestive fire, for emotional balance, to heal the reproductive organs, and to increase blood circulation.

CAVANSITE: Use at the 4th Chakra (Heart Chakra) or at the 5th Chakra (Throat Chakra) to facilitate deep emotional healing, to connect you with the energies of the sea and the water element, to enhance your ability to express love by means of creative endeavors, to stimulate compassion and create a gentle and nurturing attitude, and to clear and balance your chakra system.

CELADONITE: Use at the 4th Chakra (Heart Chakra) to facilitate a connection with the fairy realm, to connect you with your inner child, to enhance your connection with the earth and with the plant kingdom, and to provide clarity of thought and approach a situation from the heart.

CELESTITE, BLUE: (Also known as Blue Celestine) Use at the 5th Chakra (Throat Chakra) to enhance telepathy, to facilitate communication with your spirit guides and totem animals, to stimulate the intuition, to enhance feelings of peace and compassion, to stimulate hope, to over come loss and conquer grief, to enhance group communication and aid in working toward a common goal, and to open the throat chakra to allow you to speak your inner-truth.

CERUSSITE: Use at the 1st Chakra (Root Chakra) or at the 7th Chakra (Crown Chakra) to help you to maintain a connection to the physical body and to the earth during spirit work or shamanic journeying, to open the crown chakra, to enhance meditation, and to promote spiritual ascension.

CHALCEDONY, BLACK MYSTIC: Use at the 6th Chakra (3rd Eye/Brow Chakra) or at the 7th Chakra (Crown Chakra) to stimulate intuition and psychic development, for psychic self-defense and protection, to "lock" the aura for protection against outside energies or planetary influences, to help you see the bright side even in the darkest of times, to bring balance to body, mind, and spirit, and to allow you to acknowledge and then transform your shadow side and negative aspects for the good of all beings.

CHALCEDONY, BLUE: Use at the 5th Chakra (Throat Chakra) for enhancing group cooperation and communication, to aid in telepathy, to transform negative energy into positive energy, to bring balance to the mind, body, and spirit, to enhance generosity by yourself or by others, to bring joy to any situation, to increase self confidence, to enhance enthusiasm, to stifle bad dreams, to cleanse wounds, to dispel dementia, and to regulate your circulation.

CHALCEDONY, PINK: Use at the 2nd Chakra (Sacral Chakra) or at the 4th Chakra (Heart Chakra) to aid you in recovering positive childhood memories, to aid in healing afflictions of the skin, to help you to value all life (even the tiniest creature), to instill compassion toward all living things, to connect with the energies of the Goddess Quan Yin, and to balance the emotions.

CHAROITE: Use at the 6th Chakra (3rd Eye/Brow Chakra) or at the 7th Chakra (Crown Chakra) to aid on the path of spiritual service (Charoite is a wonderful stone for any energy worker, especially Reiki practitioners), to stimulate creative energies, for inner reflection, to promote a positive attitude, for protection, to keep your field clear from any energy that may otherwise be picked up from your clients during a healing session, for spiritual evolution, for spiritual healing, to promote compassion and empathy, to stimulate mystical experiences, to aid in spiritual healing, for shamanic journeying, to facilitate communication with members of the fairy realm, to increase the power of H.A.D.O or water-crystal healing, to cleanse your emotional and psychic bodies, to encourage deeper states of meditation, and to induce a feeling of peace and tranquility.

CHIASTOLITE: (Also known as Cross Stone): Use at the 1st Chakra (Root Chakra), 2nd Chakra (Sacral Chakra), or 4th Chakra (Heart Chakra) to align and balance the chakras, to balance the body, mind, and spirit, to help you manage your responsibilities, to open your heart after trauma or hurt, to instill values and ethics and help to make them a priority in your life, to lift your spirit, and to promote group cooperation.

CHRYSANTHEMUM STONE: (Also known as Flowering Gabbro) Use at any chakra to balance the flow of yin and yang energies, to allow you to see your positive and negative aspects (to aid in overcoming dependence on the ego), and to aid you in growing into your spiritual self.

CHRYSOCOLLA: (Also known as Chrysacolla, Gaia Stone, and as Venus Stone) Use at the 4th Chakra (Heart Chakra) or 5th Chakra (Throat Chakra) to connect with Goddess energy, to link the energy of the 4th Chakra (Heart Chakra) with that of the 5th Chakra (Throat Chakra) to allow you to speak from the heart, to support a deep connection with nature, to instill compassion, and to provide inner strength during difficult times.

CHRYSOCOLLA, DRUZY: (Also known as Gemmy Chrysocolla or Gem Silica) Use at the 4th Chakra (Heart Chakra) or 5th Chakra (Throat Chakra) to enhance or fine-tune these metaphysical properties of Chrysocolla. Druzy Chrysocolla can also enhance the relationship between a mother and her children or it can increase fertility in a woman trying to conceive.

CHRYSOPRASE: Use at the 4th Chakra (Heart Chakra) for encouraging hopeful attitudes, to assist in receiving truthfulness, to fuel creativity in artistic endeavors, to energize the physical body, to encourage you to become more outgoing and to take risks, to bring virtue into practice in daily life, to dispel judgmental attitudes from the self and from others, to aid in forgiveness, compassion, and empathy, to help you to communicate in a positive and encouraging matter and to enable you to give constructive criticism, to prevent bad dreams and to encourage restful sleep, to encourage spiritual ascension, to maintain a state of good physical health, to encourage self reliance, to relieve symptoms of gout, to heal the eyes, to manifest prosperity and abundance, to absorb and assimilate Vitamin C, and to relieve stress-related stomach discomfort.

CINNABAR: Use at the 1st Chakra (Root Chakra) to stimulate vitality, to aid in manifesting prosperity and abundance, to enhance the feng shui energy in your environment, to open and protect the root chakra, to treat disorders of the blood and internal organs, and to help spice up your love life.

CITRINE: Use at the 3rd Chakra (Solar Plexus Chakra) or at the 7th Chakra (Crown Chakra) for increasing creativity, for protection from negative energies, to activate the intuition, to manifest abundance, wealth, and prosperity, to encourage sharing, to promote joy, to increase self-esteem and confidence, to encourage a positive attitude, to enhance concentration, to overcome your fears, to increase ease of communication, to balance the emotions, to instill inner-strength to diminish symptoms from Chronic Fatigue Syndrome, to help eye problems, to help with blood circulation, to relieve menstrual or digestive problems, and to balance the thyroid.

CONCRETION, FAIRY STONE: (Also known as Fairy Stone) Use at the 6th Chakra (3rd Eye/Brow Chakra) as a portal between worlds, to call on the fairies to help your wishes come true, to facilitate communication with beings from the fairy realm (i.e. fairies, sprites, nymphs, ents, etc.), for grounding, to bring magic back into your love life, and to encourage a sense of peace and calming in the user.

COPPER: Use at the 1st Chakra (Root Chakra) and 2nd Chakra (Sacral Chakra) for aiding in motivation, to increase self-love, to encourage an optimistic attitude, for an increase in confidence, to overcome negative thought patterns and conditioning, to create balance between the physical and ethereal bodies, to stimulate telepathy, for good luck, for grounding, to amplify energy and intention, to maintain proper circulation, to relieve infection, and to treat arthritis pain.

CORAL, RED: Use at the 1st Chakra (Root Chakra) to increase vitality, for grounding, to enhance spiritual devotion, to heal the physical body, for protection from negative energy, and to facilitate communication with your ancestors.

CREEDITE: Use at the 2nd Chakra (Sacral Chakra) to allow you to work through your emotions safely and naturally, to connect you with the element of water to wash away feelings and thoughts that need to be released, for energetic cleansing and purification of the emotional body, to shield and protect a delicate or sensitive Sacral Chakra, to aid you in recovering (physically, mentally, spiritually, emotionally) after someone has invaded your space or depleted your energy (consciously or subconsciously), and to aid you in learning how to deflect a psychic attack.

CROCIDOLITE, LION'S SKIN: (Also known as Lion's Skin) Use at the 1st Chakra (Root Chakra), 2nd Chakra (Sacral Chakra), or at the 3rd Chakra (Solar Plexus Chakra) for courage, to enhance personal power, to regain your power when you have given it away to another (willingly or not), to heal the physical body (especially the flesh), for quick reflexes, and to enhance alertness.

CUPRITE: Use at the 1st Chakra (Root Chakra) or at the 4th Chakra (Heart Chakra) to increase fertility, for healing problems associated with the female reproductive organs, to promote feelings of safety, to aid girls in the process of becoming women (and in other rites of passage), and to heal emotional wounds (especially those that are lingering from past lives).

-D-

DANBURITE, COLORLESS: Use at the 4th Chakra (Heart Chakra), the 6th Chakra (3rd Eye/Brow Chakra), or at the 7th Chakra (Crown Chakra) to open the heart to divine love, to stimulate intuitive insight, to facilitate and enhance meditation, and to open the crown chakra.

DIAMOND, BLUE: Use at the 5th Chakra (Throat Chakra) to enhance spiritual communication, to aid in the ascension process, for purification, to motivate you in creative endeavors, for inspiration, increases good health and well-being, and to stimulate will power and inner-strength.

DIAMOND, CLEAR: Use at the 7th Chakra (Crown Chakra) for purification, to aid in the ascension process, to aid in keeping your commitments, as a reminder of your responsibilities to you as well as to others, for clarity of mind, to accelerate your karmic release, and to aid in achieving karmic liberation.

DIOPSIDE, BLACK STAR: Use at the 1st Chakra (Root Chakra), at the 6th Chakra (3rd Eye/Brow Chakra), or at the 7th Chakra (Crown Chakra) to promote mystical experiences, to encourage inner-reflection, to stimulate psychic activity, to awaken the dream consciousness while in the waking state, and to aid in connecting you with the Universe and all that is.

DIOPTASE: Use at the 4th Chakra (Heart Chakra) to balance the male and female energies of the body, to open the heart chakra to new relationships or experiences while keeping it fully protected (Dioptase has been called a supreme heart healer), to aid in the grieving process, to aid you in manifesting for your highest good, to help you work through deep emotional issues, to heal disorders of the heart, for emotional balance, to heal past life trauma, to connect with beings from the fairy realm, and to promote self-love and self-forgiveness.

DOLOMITE: Use at the 3rd Chakra (Solar Plexus Chakra) or at the 4th Chakra (Heart Chakra) to provide inner strength and will power, to help you to remain firm in your boundaries even when it is very difficult (as in a parent showing "tough love" to a child), to aid those who are oversensitive in not taking things personally, and to help to strengthen and heal a broken heart.

DRAGON STONE: Use at the 1st Chakra (Root Chakra) or 4th Chakra (Heart Chakra) for cleansing and purifying the blood, to instill courage and bravery, to physically and emotionally heal the heart, to increase vitality and strength, for power, to bring luck, to increase knowledge and wisdom, and for protection. PLEASE NOTE: Dragon Stone is a newly discovered form of Bloodstone from South Africa.

DUMORTIERITE: (Also known as Blue Quartz or as Dumortierite Quartz) Use at the 5th Chakra (Throat Chakra) or at the 6th Chakra (3rd Eye/Brow Chakra) for promoting peace and tranquility, to enhance your creativity, to enhance your organizational skills, to instill mental clarity, to increase intuitive wisdom, to promote happiness and joy, to cool anger, to facilitate a connection with your Spirit Guides or Totem Animals, to connect you with the water element and help you to "go with the flow," to reduce fever, and to cleanse the blood.

-E-

ELESTRA: (This stone is Elestial Quartz with Lepidocrocite inclusions) Use at the 6th Chakra (3rd Eye/Brow Chakra) or 7th Chakra (Crown Chakra) for enhancing love, for instilling integrity, to enhance clarity of mind, and to increase joy.

EMERALD: (Also known as Green Beryl) Use at the 4th Chakra (Heart Chakra) for bringing peace and calming, for inspiration, to bring loyalty to a relationship or to attract a loyal partner, to encourage friendship, to balance the mind, body, and spirit, to enhance love, to balance the mind, body, and spirit, to transform negative energy into positive energy, to enhance psychic powers, to stimulate empathy, for protection, to enhance memory, to aid in positive expression of the self, to stimulate group cooperation, to treat infection, to heal the eyes, to enhance a connection with the earth, to lessen to symptoms of diabetes, and to aid in relieving joint pain caused by arthritis.

EPIDOTE: Use at the 4th Chakra (Heart Chakra) for disintegrating negative energy and replacing it with positive energy, to aid in relieving symptoms associated with neurological disorders, to reduce headache pain, to aid in facilitating a connection with nature (especially with trees and flowers), and to help calm the nervous system (especially when you are experiencing anxiety, panic attack, or a great deal of stress).

EUCLASE: Use at the 4th Chakra (Heart Chakra) and at the 5th Chakra (Throat Chakra) to instill joy and happiness, to promote intuitive awareness, to cleanse and purify all of the meridians and energy channels in the body, to stimulate creativity, to enhance your passion for life, to aid in manifesting all things physical, mental, and spiritual, and to aid in meditation.

EUDIALYTE: Use at the 4th Chakra (Heart Chakra) for inner-strength, to promote respect for the inner-self, to encourage new love to grow, to attract angelic beings, to nurture the inner-self, to enhance your feminine qualities, and for emotional healing and balance.

-F-

FLUORITE, BLUE: (Also known as Blue Fluor Spar) Use at the 5th Chakra (Throat Chakra) to connect you with beings from the angelic realm, to heal problems associated with the throat chakra (especially of the thyroid gland), to open you to receiving healing energy from angelic beings, to reduce stress caused by electromagnetic frequencies, and to connect one with the element of water (for cleansing, emotional healing, etc.).

FLUORITE, COLORLESS: (Also known as Colorless Fluor Spar) Use at the 7th Chakra (Crown Chakra) for ultimate clarity of thought, to facilitate necessary changes in body temperature (i.e. to reduce fever or to warm the body after a cold spell), to enhance communication with your spirit guides (especially with Norse deities), and to bring the light of the divine into the heart.

FLUORITE, GREEN: (Also known as Green Flour Spar) Use at the 4th Chakra (Heart Chakra), 6th Chakra (3rd Eye/Brow Chakra), or at the 7th Chakra (Crown Chakra) to enhance focus and concentration (especially while studying or while learning new skills), for healing the physical body, to reduce to reduce physical stress caused by electromagnetic frequencies, to open your heart chakra, and to allow you to love and to trust others.

FLUORITE, LAVENDER: (Also known as Fluor Spar, Lavender) Use at the 7th Chakra (Crown Chakra) to disintegrate negative energy and to replace it with positive energy, for purification and protection, to reduce to protect you from electromagnetic frequencies, to aid in opening the crown chakra, to aid you in seeing your own divine nature, to enhance meditation, to access the energies of the Violet Flame, and to aid you in connecting with your spirit guides, angels, or totem animals.

FLUORITE, PURPLE: (Also known as Purple Fluor Spar) Use at the 7th Chakra (Crown Chakra) for clarity of mind, to help you focus (especially for students who are studying), to relax stiff muscles, to relieve lower back pain, to reduce inflammation caused by sprained joints, to relieve the pain of tension headaches, and to relieve symptoms associated with chemotherapy treatments.

FLUORITE, RAINBOW: (Also known as Rainbow Fluor Spar) Use at the 6th Chakra (3rd Eye/Brow Chakra) or at the 7th Chakra (Crown Chakra) for protection, to block electromagnetic pollution, to reduce stress, to transform negative energy into positive energy, for maintaining balance in the physical body, to strengthen the intuition, to improve concentration, to promote confidence in you, to improve coordination, to dispel mental illness, to show the truth in any situation, to aid in objectivity and fair judgment, to balance the emotional body, to relieve symptoms of infection, to protect against viruses, to stimulate the intellect, to enhance clarity of mind and lucidity, to stimulate relief of stiff joints, to relieve arthritis pain, to cleanse the mind, body, and spirit, to help heal injuries of the spine, to protect you from electromagnetic frequencies, to diminish pain related to the nervous system, to heal blemishes and other skin problems, to encourage accurate psychic readings, and to treat unhealthy bone marrow.

FLUORITE, YELLOW: (Also known as Yellow Fluor Spar) Use at the 3rd Chakra (Solar Plexus Chakra) to fight illness or infection, for purification of the internal organs, to protect the aura and subtle bodies, to enhance self confidence, to instill joy and happiness, to bring financial abundance, to bring the warmth of the sun into the body, to protect you from electromagnetic frequencies, to ease the symptoms of S.A.D. (Seasonal Affective Disorder), to relieve depression and anxiety, and to promote healthy digestion.

FOSSIL: Use at the 1st Chakra (Root Chakra), 2nd Chakra (Sacral Chakra), 3rd Chakra (Solar Plexus Chakra), or at the 4th Chakra (Heart Chakra) to enhance your connection with nature and its flora and fauna, to facilitate shamanic journeying, to give you access to past life memories and the Akashic records, to facilitate communication with your Spirit Guides and Totem Animals, for protection, for grounding, and to connect you with Earth energies.

FOSSIL, AMMONITE: (Also known as Ammonite) Use at the 1st Chakra (Root Chakra), 2nd Chakra (Sacral Chakra), 3rd Chakra (Solar Plexus Chakra), or 6th Chakra (3rd Eye/Brow Chakra) to enhance fertility, to connect with the energies of the mother goddess, to aid in past life recall, to enhance shamanic journeying, to aid you in connecting with your ancestors to receive guidance, to expand your conscious awareness, to facilitate a connection with the animal kingdom, to aid in animal communication, and to allow you to reap the full benefit of meditation.

FOSSIL, BRYOZOAN: Use at the 1st Chakra (Root Chakra) or at the 5th Chakra (Throat Chakra) to relieve symptoms associated with allergies, to aid you in getting from one place to another (physically, emotionally, and spiritually), to encourage personal growth, and to provide support in difficult times.

FOSSIL, CORAL: (Also known as Fossil Coral, Coral Fossil, or as Petoskey Stone) Use at the 1st Chakra (Root Chakra) or at the 2nd Chakra (Sacral Chakra) for enhancing your connection with nature, to promote relaxation, to tap into ancient wisdom, to enhance your physical health, and to increase mental and physical strength. PLEASE NOTE: This is only known as Petoskey Stone if its origin is Michigan.

FOSSIL, CORAL RED AGATIZED HORN: Use at the 1st Chakra (Root Chakra) or at the 4th Chakra (Heart Chakra) to instill a sense of bravery in the user, to summon the courage to do new and unfamiliar things, and to help heal disorders of the blood.

FOSSIL, DINOSAUR EGGSHELL: Use at the 1st Chakra (Root Chakra) or at the 6th Chakra (3rd Eye/Brow Chakra) to access the Akashic Records, to facilitate communication with your ancestors in order to receive guidance or information, to enhance fertility, to encourage growth (physical, mental, or spiritual), to assist you in making new breakthroughs in life, and for enhancing your sense of independence.

FOSSIL, PETRIFIED WOOD: Use at the 1st Chakra (Root Chakra) for grounding, to enhance your connection with nature (especially with ents, tree spirits, and members of the fairy realm), to aid in accessing ancient wisdom, for protection, and to aid in past life ascension.

FOSSIL, SAGE BRUSH: Use at the 1st Chakra (Root Chakra), 2nd Chakra (Sacral Chakra), 3rd Chakra (Solar Plexus Chakra), 6th Chakra (3rd

Eye/Brow Chakra), or 7th Chakra (Crown Chakra) for purification, to remove negative energies and replace them with positivity, for protection of your space, and to connect you with the spirit of the plant realm.

FOSSIL, SEA URCHIN: Use at the 1st Chakra (Root Chakra), 2nd Chakra (Sacral Chakra), 4th Chakra (Heart Chakra), or at the 5th Chakra (Throat Chakra) to promote feelings of peace and calming, to connect you with the water element, to promote a feeling of lightness when surrounded by heavy or negative energies, for healing the musculoskeletal system, and to aid you in accessing the Akashic Records.

FOSSIL, SHARK TOOTH: Use at the 5th Chakra (Throat Chakra) to relieve pain associated with the teeth and gums, to connect you with ancestors, to remember your past lives, and to promote strong bone growth.

FOSSIL, STROMATOLITE BUTTON: Use at the 1st Chakra (Root Chakra), 2nd Chakra (Sacral Chakra), or at the 3rd Chakra (Solar Plexus Chakra) to help fight bacterial and fungal infections, to aid in personal growth, to help you to get past another's harsh exterior to understand the person at your core, to encourage new love to grow, to help women to see and appreciate their divine feminine power, to connect you with the energy of the Virgin of Guadalupe, and to aid in healing past life trauma.

FOSSIL, TRILOBITE: Use at the 1st Chakra (Root Chakra) or at the 5th Chakra (Throat Chakra) to promote change and adaptability (especially in those with stubborn personalities), for helping you to stay afloat in troubled waters, to enhance your knowledge and wisdom, and to help you to return to your roots.

FUCHSITE: (Also known as Green Mica) Use at the 4th Chakra (Heart Chakra) to aid you in appreciating the beauty in all things, to open the heart to feelings of goodwill toward all beings, to add a sense of magic and wonder to your time with your children, and to attract fairies and sprites.

-G-

GAIA STONE: (Also known as Green Obsidian) Use at the 4th Chakra (Heart Chakra) to enhance your connection with nature and with Mother Earth herself, to encourage love and compassion for all beings, to enhance all earth healing practices, to facilitate communication with beings of the animal and plant realms, to open nyour heart and mind to the importance of environmental activism, to encourage you to "think globally and act locally", and to promote harmony and balance for the good of all beings in the universe.

GALENA: (Also known as Lead Ore) Use at the 1st Chakra (Root Chakra) for aiding in grounding during shamanic journey work or astral travel, for protection of the astral body while journeying, to maintain a connection with the inner self, and to facilitate communication with animals.

GARNET, ANDRADITE BLACK: (Also known as Melanite) Use at the 1st Chakra (Root Chakra) or at the 6th Chakra (3rd Eye/Brow Chakra) for grounding, for protection of the energy body from psychic attack, to stimulate your clairvoyant abilities (psychic sight), to heal disorders of the liver, to facilitate trance states (especially for channeling), and to provide a window into the Akashic Records to learn about past, present, and future.

GARNET, DEMANTOID GREEN: Use at the 3rd Chakra (Solar Plexus Chakra) or at the 4th Chakra (Heart Chakra) to connect you with beings form the fairy realm, to aid you in seeing the beauty and magic of trees, to aid you in developing a great appreciation of nature, to enhance your knowledge and understanding of the plant kingdom (especially herbalism), to shield and protect the heart chakra from outside energies, to heal the emotional body, and for protection from envy or jealousy (either from having these feelings toward others or vice versa).

GARNET, GROSSULAR GREEN: (Also known as Green Grossularite) Use at the 3rd Chakra (Solar Plexus Chakra) or at the 4th Chakra (Heart Chakra) to open chakras that have been shut down while keeping them protected; to shield the aura from negativity; to enhance prosperity; to aid in relieving stomach discomfort; to overcome major life obstacles; to reduce arthritis pain; and to bring wealth and prosperity to the user.

GARNET, GROSSULAR PINK: (Also known as Pink Grossularite) Use at the 2nd Chakra (Sacral

Chakra) or at the 4th Chakra (Heart Chakra) to open chakras that have been shut down while keeping them protected; to shield the aura from negativity by transmuting negative energy into loving energy; to balance the emotions; to reduce pain and inflammation; and to enhance feelings of compassion and empathy.

GARNET, HESSIONITE: (Also known as Cinnamon Stone or as Peach Garnet) Use at the 1st Chakra (Root Chakra) or at the 2nd Chakra (Sacral Chakra) to balance the emotional body, to increase the positive and to balance the negative aspects of your astrological sign, to bring out your masculine energies, and to aid you in connecting with your higher self.

GARNET, PYROPE RED: Use at the 1st Chakra (Root Chakra) or at the 4th Chakra (Heart Chakra) to stimulate vitality, to treat sluggish digestion and to increase your digestive fire, to increase motivation, to instill self-confidence, to promote spiritual ascension, and to manifest prosperity and abundance.

GARNET, RHODOLITE RED VIOLET: Use at the 1st Chakra (Root Chakra) or at the 7th Chakra (Crown Chakra) to cleanse and purify the blood, to enhance prosperity and abundance, to stimulate vitality and enhance your life force energy, to bring clarity of mind, to encourage spiritual exploration, to enhance meditation, and to bring your spiritual consciousness into the physical realm.

GARNET, SPESSARTINE: (Also known as Spessartite or as Garnet, Orange) Use at the

1st Chakra (Root Chakra) or at the 2nd Chakra (Sacral Chakra) to stimulate vitality, to enhance sexual energy and desire, to help stimulate proper circulation, to aid in animal communication, and to connect you with your totem animals.

GARNET, UVAROVITE: (Also known as Garnet, Green) Use at the 1st Chakra (Root Chakra) or at the 4th Chakra (Heart Chakra) to connect you with nature (the elements, nature spirits, and Mother Earth herself), to instill a sense of compassion for all beings, for earth healing, to re-open the heart chakra after hurt or heartbreak, and to shield your aura from negativity.

GASPEITE: Use at the 3rd Chakra (Solar Plexus Chakra) or at the 4th Chakra (Heart Chakra) to ease digestive complaints, to facilitate a connection with the inner child and to project love to him or her, for enhancing communication with plants and animals as well as nature spirits and fairies, to rid you of toxic energies and negative traits.

GLENDONITE: (Also known as Calcite Pseudomorph after Ikaite) Use at the 2nd Chakra (Sacral Chakra) or at the 3rd Chakra (Solar plexus Chakra) for providing support and emotional stability, for mental clarity, to help you learn new things, and as a gentle reminder to spend time on personal healing.

GOETHITE: Use at the 1st Chakra (Root Chakra) for protection of the astral body during astral travel, to enhance meditation, for instilling a sense of non-attachment to the physical realm, to enhance the connection with your inner self, and for removing blockages in the upper chakras.

GOLD: Use at the 3rd Chakra (Solar Plexus Chakra) or at the 7th Chakra (Crown Chakra) to balance masculine and feminine energies, to bring the energy of the sun into the body, to warm the body, to open the crown chakra, to promote a willingness to change (to be malleable), to balance the hormones, and to aid you in overcoming addictions.

GYPSUM DESERT ROSE: (Also known as Selenite Desert Rose) Use at the 3rd Chakra (Solar Plexus Chakra) or at the 7th Chakra (Crown Chakra) to facilitate a connection with the earth element, to open your conscious awareness into a state of divine bliss and Christ-like consciousness, to treat wounds and sores of the skin, and to facilitate the blossoming of your lotus mind into enlightenment.

-H-

HALITE, BLUE: Use at the 6th Chakra (3rd Eye/Brow Chakra) or at the 7th Chakra (Crown Chakra) for purification of the subtle bodies, to enhance psychic awareness, to cut your energetic cords and connections, to enhance your channeling abilities, to connect you to the energies of the archangels (especially with Archangel Metatron), and to stimulate conscious awareness.

HALITE, PINK: Use at the 4th Chakra (Heart Chakra) to disintegrate negative energy and replace it with positive energy, to create a barrier of protection around the heart chakra and to shield a sensitive heart from outside influences, to heal the emotional body, to remove past hurts and to heal old wounds, to encourage attitudes of forgiveness and understanding, to heal damaged friendships or relationships, and to create a positive environment for children.

HEALER'S GOLD: Use this powerful combination of Pyrite & Magnetite at at 3rd Chakra (Solar Plexus Chakra) or at the 7th Chakra (Crown Chakra) to enhance the vibration of energy channeled to clients during a healing session, to raise the energetic vibration of a healing space or sacred space, to call in beneficial helpers (i.e. guardian angels, spirit guides, totem animals, etc.) during a healing session, and to facilitate the continued healing of the client even after the session has ended.

HELIODOR: (Also known as Golden Beryl or as Yellow Beryl) Use at the 3rd Chakra (Solar Plexus Chakra) to relieve symptoms of Seasonal Affective Disorder (S.A.D.), to enhance self-confidence, to instill joy in the user, to heal grief, and to banish fears of all kinds.

HEMATITE: (Also known as Kidney Ore or as Bloodstone) Use at the 1st Chakra (Root Chakra) for grounding, to balance the mind, body, and spirit, for astral travel and shamanic journeying, to transform negative energy into positive energy, to bring peace and calming, to encourage confidence, to aid in removing addictions, to aid in acceptance of your life, to increase concentration, to stimulate memory, to encourage creativity, for inner-reflection, for protection, for pain relief, to aid in curbing materialism, to aid in studying, to maintain proper blood circulation, to help the body assimilate iron, to relieve insomnia, and to reduce fever. PLEASE NOTE: Hematite is only known as Kidney Ore when it appears in its botryoidal form.

HEMATITE, GOLDEN RUTILATED: Use at the 1st Chakra (Root Chakra) or at the 7th Chakra (Crown Chakra) to balance the yin and yang energies in the body, to bring the universal healing light to any situation, and to connect you with celestial and planetary energies.

HEMATITE, SPECULAR: Use at the 1st Chakra (Root Chakra), 6th Chakra (3rd Eye/Brow Chakra), or at the 7th Chakra (Crown Chakra) to aid you in contemplating the mysteries of the universe, to encourage positive or discourage negative planetary influences, to enhance the positive attributes of your zodiac sign, and to facilitate astral travel while maintaining a grounded connection with the earth.

HEMIMORPHITE, BLUE: Use at the 5th Chakra (Throat Chakra) to bring the energies of the oceans and the sea into the physical body, to aid in releasing emotional blockages, to wash away habits and patterns that are no longer serving your highest good, to instill a sense of child-like wonder that may be unfamiliar to you or that you have forgotten as an adult, and to aid you in releasing fears resulting fro negative or traumatizing past-life experiences.

HEULANDITE, GREEN: Use at the 1st Chakra (Root Chakra) or at the 4th Chakra (Heart Chakra) to allow excess heart energy to flow out to the universe for the good of all beings, to heal physical problems associated with bacterial and fungal infections, to open the heart in a protected manner, to slow the growth of cancerous cells, to aid you in ridding the body of toxins and excess fats, and to promote general healing of the physical body.

HEULANDITE, PINK: Use at the 2nd Chakra (Sacral Chakra) or at the 4th Chakra (Heart Chakra) to aid you in becoming more gentle (in your actions as well as words), to heal problems associated with the stomach or with the digestive tract (especially those associated with acid or bile production), to allow you to realize your potential (without the presence of the ego), to bring balance and harmony during stressful times, and to provide support while making difficult decisions.

HIDDENITE: (Also known as Green Spodumene) Use at the 3rdChakra (Solar Plexus Chakra) or at the 4th Chakra (Heart Chakra) to instill a sense of compassion for all beings, to encourage the user to act with Lovingkindness (even in difficult or frustrating situations), to promote joy and a sense of child-like wonder, to remind you to be grateful for the small things in life to remove stress, to promote flexibility of mind *and* body (especially for yoga), and to aid you in developing a new outlook on a situation or to understand the opposing viewpoint of a conflict or argument.

HOLY STONE: (Also known as Mongolian Magic Stone or as Holey Stone) Use this stone at any chakra as just having this stone within your aura dissolves energetic blockages and open all chakras and meridians within the subtle bodies. It may also be used for cleansing and purification, to remove toxins from the body (especially from sensitive internal organs), to remove physical and emotional pain, and to connect you with your ancestors.

HOWLITE: Use at the 6th Chakra (3rd Eye/Brow Chakra) or at the 7th Chakra (Crown Chakra) for enhancing lucid dreaming practices, to banish nightmares and encourage "sweet dreams," to aid you in feeling rested after sleep, to enhance your ability to recall your dreams, to open the 6th Chakra (3rd Eye/Brow Chakra) to stimulate intuition and psychic awareness, and to promote feelings of oneness with all beings.

HYPERSTHENE: Use at the 6th Chakra (3rd Eye/Brow Chakra) to remove entity attachments, for protection from psychic attack, to shield your energy body from negative energy, and to fill your auric field with positivity.

-I-

INFINITE: (Also known as Infinite Serpentine) Use at the 3rdChakra (Solar Plexus Chakra) and at the 4th Chakra (Heart Chakra) to facilitate communication with beings of the fairy realm, to establish a deep-rooted connection with nature, to protect you against illness (especially from the flu), to relieve symptoms of the common cold, for renewal (physical, mental, and spiritual), for general healing, and to aid you in getting a fresh start.Infinite is a variety of Serpentine.

IOLITE: (Also known as Water Sapphire, Cordierite, and Viking's Compass) Use at the 5th Chakra (Throat Chakra) or 6th Chakra (3rd Eye/Brow Chakra) to aid in direction and guidance (physical and spiritual), to instill hope, to promote feelings of peace, calming, and tranquility, to aid in communication with your inner-self, as a companion stone for journeying activities, and to heal the body, mind, and spirit.

IRONSTONE: Use at the 1st Chakra (Root Chakra) or at the 2nd Chakra (Sacral Chakra) for grounding, to connect you with your ancestors, for earth healing, to aid in cloud busting or shifting weather, to enhance creativity, to help you realize the beauty in all things.

-J-

JADE, BLUE: Use at the 4th Chakra (Heart Chakra) or 5th Chakra (Throat Chakra) to enhance group communication and cooperation, to connect the heart chakra with the throat chakra allowing you to speak your inner truth, to bring good fortune, to enhance creativity, to stimulate success in business endeavors, and to bring peace and calming during chaotic situations.

JASPER, BRECCIATED: Use at the 1st Chakra (Root Chakra) to aid in sorting through details, to pull the pieces of your life together, to aid in strengthening friendships and family bonds, to aid in the soul retrieval process, and to enhance shamanic journeying work.

JADE, GREEN: Use at the 4th Chakra (Heart Chakra) for gaining wisdom and insight through meditation, to bring love and compassion, for protection, to bring mind, body, and spirit into balance, to bring luck, to stimulate new friendships, to encourage independence, to stimulate creativity, to bring intuitive dreams, to bring peace and calming, to cleanse the physical body, to increase fertility, to aid in successful child birth, for healing the physical body, to manifest wealth and prosperity, for personal growth, and to bring balance to the systems of the physical body.

JADE, HUNAN: Use at the 1st Chakra (Root Chakra) or at the 4th Chakra (Heart Chakra) to aid in personal development and growth, to aid in Heart Chakra healing, to promote inner peace, to encourage compassionate attitudes, to help you find stillness during meditation, and to encourage Buddha-like attitudes.

JADEITE, GREEN: (Also known as Green Jadeite Jade) Use at the 4th Chakra (Heart Chakra) to disintegrate negative energy, to heal the physical body, to aid in manifesting abundance (physical and spiritual), for protection (especially of women an children), and to remove obstacles on your path to enlightenment.

JASPER, DALMATIAN: (Also known as Dalmatian Dacite) Use at the 1st Chakra (Root Chakra) to promote a connection with nature, to enhance your ability to communicate with animals and to aid in communication with your spirit guides and totem animals.

JASPER, FANCY: (Also known as Rainbow Jasper) Use at the lower chakras; 1st Chakra (Root Chakra), 2nd Chakra (Sacral Chakra), 3rd Chakra (Solar Plexus Chakra); 4th Chakra (Heart Chakra) for encouraging peace and calming, promoting group cooperation, to aid in grounding, to assist with shamanic journeying and dreaming exercises, for balance in the mind, body, and spirit, to promote emotional strength, to activate creativity, to aid in circulation of the blood, and to increase positive thinking. This is a low quality form of Ocean Jasper.

JASPER, GARY GREEN: (Also known as Green Bogwood, Green Larsonite, McDermitt Green Jasper, Gary Green Larsonite Jasper, McDermitt Green Larsonite Jasper, Green Larsenite, or as Green Larsonite Jasper) Use at the 1st Chakra (Root Chakra) or at the 4th Chakra (Heart Chakra) for absorbing positive vibrations from the universe, to aid you in feeling safe and protected by mother nature, to protect you from illness, to facilitate a connection with nature (especially with tree spirits and other members of the plant kingdom), to help you to stay afloat while in troubled waters (physical, emotional, or spiritual), and to heal and balance the energy of the heart chakra.

JASPER, IVORY: Use at the 2nd Chakra (Sacral Chakra) for good luck, to promote compassionate attitudes, for group cooperation, and to connect with the energy of the elephant totem animal.

JASPER, KAMBABA: Use at the 1st Chakra (Root Chakra) or at the 4th Chakra (Heart Chakra) to enhance your connection with nature, to facilitate a connection to beings of the Fairy Realm, to enhance meditation, to instill Lovingkindness and compassion, and to promote peace and calming.

JASPER, LEOPARD SKIN: (Also known as Leopard Stone, Leopard Skin Rhyolite or as Leopard Skin Rhyolite Jasper) Use at the 1st Chakra (Root Chakra) or 2nd Chakra (Sacral Chakra) for manifesting healing energies, to increase energy in the etheric body, to maintain proper health in the systems of the body, to increase your personal strengths, to bring balance to mind, body, and sprit, to banish negative energies, to aid in the assimilation of nutrients, to bring peace and calming, to encourage a helping hand both to and from others, to stimulate shamanic journeying and astral travel, for protection, to cleanse the etheric body, to banish electromagnetic pollution, to facilitate accurate pendulum dowsing sessions, to bring will power, to stimulate courage, to increase organization of your environment, to bring support during times of illness, and to stimulate cognition.

JASPER, MARBLE: Use at the 1st Chakra (Root Chakra) or at the 5th Chakra (Throat Chakra) to aid in nutrient absorption, to bring balance to the body, to instill attitudes of gratitude, and to promote sweet and kind attitudes of compassion.

JASPER, MOOKAITE: (Also known as Mookaite, as Mookite, and as Mookite Jasper) Use at the 1st Chakra (Root Chakra), at the 2nd Chakra (Sacral Chakra), or at the 3rd Chakra (Solar Plexus Chakra) to instill creativity, for emotional balance and healing, to encourage a healthy expression of the emotions through art or music, to help lift the fog that doubt can sometimes cast over areas of your life, to promote kind attitudes, and to help ground you by connecting you to earth energy.

JASPER, ORBICULAR: (Also known as Ocean Jasper, as Orbicular Rhyolite, as Ocean Rhyolite, or as Atlantis Stone) Use at the 1st Chakra (Root Chakra), 4th Chakra (Heart Chakra) or 6th Chakra (3rd Eye/Brow Chakra) Use at the 1st Chakra (Root Chakra), 4th Chakra (Heart Chakra) or 6th Chakra (3rd Eye/Brow Chakra) for establishing a connection with the earth and with the sea, for accessing the Akashic records, to connect you with ancient civilizations, to access ancient wisdom and knowledge, to instill joy, to promote a positive attitude, and for healing and balancing of the mind, body, and spirit.

JASPER, PICASSO: (Also known as Picasso Stone or as Picasso Marble) Use at the 2nd Chakra (Sacral Chakra) or at the 5th Chakra (Throat Chakra) to stimulate your creative energies, for inspiration, to aid in overcoming your current life challenges, to facilitate communication (especially when expressing you about difficult situations or feelings), for inner harmony, and to aid you in the ability to receive divine insight.

JASPER, PICTURE: (Also known as Kalahari Jasper, Kalahari Desert Jasper or as Kalahari Picture Jasper) Use at the 1st Chakra (Root Chakra) and 2nd Chakra (Sacral Chakra) to aid you in seeing the beauty in all things, to stimulate your creative energy, to enhance visualization exercises, to connect you with a specific place or time, to promote clarity of mind, to enhance meditation, and to bring inner peace and harmony.

JASPER, POLYCHROME: Use at any chakra to balance and align the energy body, to stimulate creative energy (especially for painters), to encourage you to change and shift with your circumstances in order to produce a favorable outcome for yourself, to enhance meditation, to instill a sense of tranquility, and to induce zen-like states in which the user achieves an "empty" state of mind.

JASPER, RAINFOREST: (Also known as Rainforest Rhyolite or as Rainforest Rhyolite Jasper) Use at the 1st Chakra (Root Chakra) and the 4th Chakra (Heart Chakra) to promote a connection with nature, to enhance a "green thumb" and to expand your knowledge of the plant kingdom (especially of herbalism), to instill respect for all living things, to connect you with Gaia (the Earth Mother), to stimulate creativity, and to enhance love and trust in a relationship.

JASPER, RED: Use at the 1st Chakra (Root Chakra) for grounding, to encourage justice, to stimulate intuitive insight to your problems and life challenges, to aid in remembering your dreams, to aid in the process of reincarnation-providing a more favorable rebirth, to aid in asserting your personal boundaries, to detoxify the blood, to regulate circulation, to bring peace and calming, to encourage a helping hand both to and from others, to stimulate shamanic journeying and astral travel, for protection, to cleanse the etheric body, to banish electromagnetic pollution, to facilitate accurate pendulum dowsing sessions, to treat sluggish digestion and to increase your digestive fire, to bring will power, to stimulate courage, to increase organization of your environment, to bring support during times of illness, & to stimulate cognition.

JASPER, SCENIC: Use at the 2nd Chakra (Sacral Chakra) or at the 5th Chakra (Throat Chakra) to enhance creativity, to banish behaviors of procrastination, to aid in manifesting abundance, and to bring hopes or ideas into fruition.

JASPER, STARRY: Use at the 1st Chakra (Root Chakra) or at the 3rd Chakra (Solar Plexus Chakra) to connect you with beings from the sky and the heavens, to promote safe astral travel, for healing on a karmic and soul level, and to encourage you to let your inner light shine.

JASPER, YELLOW: Use at the 3rd Chakra (Solar Plexus Chakra) to instill confidence, to promote inner strength, to increase vitality, to manifest abundance, to counter act the symptoms of Seasonal Affective Disorder (SAD), to aid in developing your talents and personal gifts, to bring happiness to children, for personal protection, to protect the aura and energetic bodies, to aid in digestion, to enhance creativity when beginning new projects, and to help you to see the bright side of any situation.

JET: (Also known as Black Amber or as Witches' Amber) Use at the 1st Chakra (Root Chakra), the 2nd Chakra (Sacral Chakra), or at the 6th Chakra

(Third Eye Chakra) to balance the male and female energies within your body, to connect you with your ancestors, to promote mystical experience, to enhance intuition and psychic skills, to open/awaken the Third Eye Chakra, to aid you in learning to appreciate nature and the plant kingdom, to instill respect for all things ancient (as well as for the elderly), and to boost your energy and overall vitality. Jet is often seen as a companion stone to Amber, with Amber representing masculine energy and Jet representing feminine energy.

-K-

KUNZITE: (Also known as Pink Spodumene) Use at the 2nd Chakra (Sacral Chakra) or at the 4th Chakra (Heart Chakra) to promote a feeling of safety, to encourage Lovingkindness, for emotional healing, to provide emotional protection, and to enhance a spiritual connection with Universal energies.

KYANITE, BLACK: (Also known as Black Disthene and as Black Cyanite) Use at the 1st Chakra (Root Chakra) or 6th Chakra (3rd Eye/Brow Chakra) for protection from negativity, to block psychic attack, for grounding, to stimulate intuitive guidance, to reduce electromagnetic pollution from electronic devices, to stimulate vivid dreams, to enhance your creativity when branching out into new endeavors, for shamanic journeying, and to promote feelings of safety and security.

KYANITE, BLUE: (Also known as Blue Disthene and as Blue Cyanite) Use at the 5th Chakra (Throat

Chakra) or 6th Chakra (3rd Eye/Brow Chakra) for spiritual guidance, to enhance your intuition, to promote peace and compassion, to stimulate creative energy, to aid in communication with your spirit guides, totem animals, and guardian angels, and to enhance your personal exploration of your spiritual nature.

KYANITE, BLUE STAR: (Also known as Blue Star Disthene or as Blue Star Cyanite) Use at the 5th Chakra (Throat Chakra), 6th Chakra (3rd Eye/Brow Chakra), or at the 7th Chakra (Crown Chakra) for bringing celestial and planetary energies into the body, to promote safe and significant astral travel, to open you to the power of divine love, and to aid you in developing your psychic awareness.

KYANITE, GREEN: (Also known as Green Disthene or as Green Cyanite) Use at the 4th Chakra (Heart Chakra) or at the 5th Chakra (Throat Chakra) to balance and align the heart and throat chakras, to repair the aura, for Earth healing, to expel negative energy from the body, to help you absorb nutrients (especially iron), and to heal problems associated with the back or spine.

KYANITE, ORANGE: Use at the 2nd Chakra (Sacral Chakra) for healing the emotional body, to provide a sense of peace and calming, for instilling creativity, for manifesting, to clear blockages from the meridians, to detox the physical body, and to enhance communication with animals.

-L-

LABRADORITE: (Also known as Spectrolite) Use at the 6th Chakra (3rd Eye/Brow Chakra) or at the 7th Chakra (Crown Chakra) for protection, to dispel negative energies, to form personal boundaries, to facilitate past life ascension or regression, to facilitate astral travel, to aid in accessing the Akashic records and other esoteric knowledge, for balancing the physical body with the etheric body, to increase conscious awareness, to facilitate intuition and psychic powers, to dispel fears, to increase faith, to strengthen trust, to facilitate mystical experiences, to stimulate the imagination and creativity, to remove illusion, to aid in acts of magic, to reveal the truth in any situation, to connect you with the Divine energy of the universe, to bring companionship, to remove stress, to treat symptoms of the common cold, to relieve arthritis pain, to regulate hormones, and to lower blood pressure.

LAPIS LAZULI: Use at the 5th Chakra (Throat Chakra) or at the 6th Chakra (3rd Eye Chakra/Brow Chakra) for facilitating spiritual enlightenment, aiding in dreaming practices, encouraging psychic power and intuition, to stimulate spiritual and shamanic journeying and astral travel, to remove stress, to bring peace and calming, for protection, to access your spirit guides such as totem animals and guardian angels, to connect you with your ancestors or for connection with ancient cultures, to banish negative energy, to aid in speaking your truth, to bring balance to the mind, body, and spirit, to dispel depression, to facilitate communication, to encourages virtuous behavior, to stimulate compassion, to increase creativity, to remove headache pain, to regulate and balance the thyroid gland, to relieve insomnia, and to boost the immune system.

LAPIS LAZULI, DENIM: Use at the 5th Chakra (Throat Chakra) or at the 6th Chakra (3rd Eye/Brow Chakra) to allow you to clearly and openly communicate with beings form the angelic realm, to help you to find your own unique voice, to enhance clairvoyance, to encourage psychic insight and intuition to aid in your decision-making process, and to prepare you for learning from the spirit/ether element.

LARIMAR: (Also known as Dolphin Stone, Blue Pectolite, or Atlantis Stone) (Also known as Blue Pectolite and Dolphin Stone) Use at the 5th Chakra (Throat Chakra) for promoting peace and calming, to stimulate emotional healing, to connect you with Goddess energy, and to promote communication with your spirit guides and totem animals.

LARVIKITE: (Also known as Silver Labradorite) Use at the 6th Chakra (3rd Eye/Brow Chakra) or at the 7th Chakra (Crown Chakra) to connect your conscious mind with beings from other dimensions, to aid in channeling, for healing of the spiritual body, to assist you in safe astral travel practices, and to shield the energy body from negativity of all kinds.

LEPIDOLITE: (Also known as Lepidolite Mica) Use at the 4th Chakra (Heart Chakra) for balance, to promote feelings of compassion, to enhance peace, calming, and tranquility during stressful times, to aid in forgiveness, to encourage harmonious relationships, to reduce to protect you from electromagnetic frequencies, to encourage feelings of comfort and safety, and to encourage new friendships to blossom.

LIBYAN DESERT GLASS: (Also known as Golden Tektite) Use at the 3rd Chakra (Solar Plexus Chakra) or at the 7th Chakra (Crown Chakra) to aid you in clearing obstacles on the path to enlightenment, to facilitate communication with your higher self, to aid in spiritual ascension, to open you to the divine, for spiritual healing, for enhancing past-life recall and remembrance of your karmic obligations or soul contracts, and to stimulate self-awareness. Libyan Desert Glass is a Tektite Meteorite.

LODESTONE: Use at the 1st Chakra (Root Chakra) for grounding and protection, to heal physical trauma, to attract a suitable partner, to aid in manifesting for the good of all beings (including the self), to attract positive people into your life, to help keep you from being drawn into negative situations, and to protect you from adverse planetary energetic influences.

-M-

MAGNETITE: Use at the 1st Chakra (Root Chakra) to attract wealth and abundance into your life, to banish negative attitudes, to promote feelings of gratitude and thankfulness for what you already have, to draw your ideal partner to you, to facilitate a connection with nature spirits, to aid you in better understanding connection with sacred geometry, and to enhance the energy body in order to raise it to a higher vibrational state.

MALACHITE: Use at the 4th Chakra (Heart Chakra) for amplifying energy and intention, for grounding, for protection, to block electromagnetic pollution, for earth healing, to connect one with nature, for spiritual guidance, to aid in visualization practices, to activate psychic powers, to encourage unconditional love, for scrying divination practices, for facilitating astral travel, to access intuitive messages from the subconscious mind, to encourage positive changes in your life, to reveal obstacles on your spiritual path, to remove negative thought patterns and conditioning, to facilitate the tactful expression of your emotions, for protection in love, to increase confidence, to encourage compassion, to enhance concentration, to heal the emotional body, to aid in exploring the inner self, to help ensure successful child birth, to treat asthma, to relieve arthritis pain, to lower blood pressure, to relieve vertigo, to strengthen the immune system, to enhance your creative energy, and to remove toxins from the body.

MERLINITE: (Also known as Psilomelane) Use at the 1st Chakra (Root Chakra) or at the 6th Chakra (3rd Eye/Brow Chakra) for stimulating mystical experiences, to strengthen the etheric cord that connects the energy bodies to the physical body, for protection in magic, to stimulate the intuition, to dissolve blockages in the energy field, to help you overcome your self-limiting beliefs, to banish unnecessary patterns and systems from your life, to transmute negative thoughts into positive thoughts, and to enhance psychic abilities.

MERLINITE, MYSTIC: Use at the 6th Chakra (3rd Eye/Brow Chakra), to enhance your magical abilities, to connect you with the wisdom of the ancient mystics and sages, for balance, to stimulate intuition and enhance your innate psychic abilities, to help heal past life trauma, to promote personal peace and to encourage self-forgiveness, and to communicate with your spirit guides, totem animals, and guardian angels.

METEORITE, CAMPO DEL CIELO: Use at the 1st Chakra (Root Chakra), the 6th Chakra (3rd Eye/Brow Chakra), or at the 7th Chakra (Crown Chakra), to connect you with your ancestors, to regain past-life memories, to facilitate shamanic journeying, to enhance astral travel and dream healing while maintaining a grounded connection to the earth, and to communicate with your spirit guides and totem animals.

METEORITE, CHONDRITE: Use at the 7th Chakra (Crown Chakra) to facilitate astral travel, to promote dream healing, to ground universal healing energy into the earth, and to enhance peaceful attitudes and behaviors.

METEORITE, SIKHOTE–ALIN: Use at the 6th Chakra (3rd Eye Chakra) or at the 7th Chakra (Crown Chakra) to facilitate astral travel, to aid in lucid dreaming, to aid you in preparing for difficult situations or experiences, and to overcome feelings of anger (belonging to you or to others).

METEORITE, TEKTITE BLACK: Use at the 1st Chakra (Root Chakra) or at the 6th Chakra (3rd Eye/Brow Chakra) for protection, to shield the aura from negativity, to promote lucid dreaming, to enhance dream recall, and to promote psychic vision.

METEORITE, TEKTITE TIBETAN: Use at the 1st Chakra (Root Chakra) or at the 7th Chakra (Crown Chakra) to facilitate communication with higher spiritual beings, to increase the benefits of astral travel, to manifest the opportunity to learn from the air element, for spiritual awakening, to allow for nonjudgmental self-reflection, and to help you to see a situation from another point of view.

MICA, BIOTITE BLACK: (Also known as Biotite, Black) Use at the 1st Chakra (Root Chakra) for grounding, for protection, to act as a mirror to allow you to see your strengths and weaknesses, to bring out the best of your astrological sign, and to connect you with your spirit guides (especially those from Egyptian mythology).

MICA, MUSCOVITE SILVER: Use at the 3rd Chakra (Solar Plexus Chakra) for self-protection, to absorb negative energy that has accumulated in the aura so that it may be cleared form your field, for inner reflection, and to shed light on the aspects of the shadow self that need to be identified and shifted.

MIMETITE: Use at the 4th Chakra (Heart Chakra) to connect you with nature and nature spirits (i.e. fairies, elves, sprites, etc.), to open the heart to new experiences, and to help you emulate your role models in order to become a better person for the good of all beings.

MOLDAVITE: (Also known as Green Tektite) Use at the 4th Chakra (Heart Chakra), 6th Chakra (3rd Eye/Brow Chakra), or 7th Chakra (Crown Chakra) for facilitating astral travel, for shamanic journeying and soul journeying, to aid you in connecting with higher beings, for facilitating spiritual ascension, to facilitate dream journeying, for enhancing intuitive powers and psychic phenomena, and for healing the mind, body, and spirit. Moldavite is a good companion stone for Herkimer Diamond Quartz. When used together, the stones will enhance each other's qualities.

MOONSTONE, BLACK: Use at the 6th Chakra (3rd Eye/Brow Chakra) to stimulate your intuition, to bring a feeling of tranquility when feeling overwhelmed or stressed, to aid you in reflecting on yourself or your relationships with others, to connect you with your feminine power or to bring balance to an overly masculine energy, and to help problems associated with cancer in the reproductive organs.

MOONSTONE, PEACH: (Also known as Apricot Moonstone) Use at the 3rd Chakra (Solar Plexus Chakra) or at the 7th Chakra (Crown Chakra) for increasing insight and intuition, to bring chaos in to order, for peace and calming, to encourage compassion, to facilitate lucid dreaming, for ceremonies and rituals pertaining to the full moon, to promote psychic powers, to increase feminine energy, to encourage your nurturing qualities, to connect you with Goddess energy, to reduce stress, to balance the emotional body and aid in emotional healing, to facilitate healing of the emotional body, to heal the female reproductive organs, to stimulate the pineal gland, to calm restless children, to aid in the assimilation of nutrients, for detoxification of the physical body, to aid in conception, to relieve insomnia, and to prevent walking in your sleep.

MOONSTONE, RAINBOW: (Also known as White Labradorite) Use at the 2nd Chakra (Sacral Chakra), the 6th Chakra (3rd Eye/Brow Chakra), or at the 7th Chakra (Crown Chakra) to enhance mystical experiences, to enhance Goddess energy, to stimulate intuitive insight, to aid in dream healing, to increase fertility, to promote a regular menstrual cycle, to facilitate lucid dreaming, and to relieve menstrual cramps and pain associated with periods (including headaches).

MOONSTONE, WHITE: Use at the 2nd Chakra (Sacral Chakra), the 4th Chakra (Heart Chakra), or at the 6th Chakra (3rd Eye/Brow Chakra) to help balance the emotions, to reduce discomfort associated with the symptoms of PMS, to ensure a pregnancy will come to term, to aid in reducing complications during childbirth, to heal the female reproductive organs, to facilitate a connection with the energies of the moon, to open you to the influences of the water element, to remove fears associated with water, for healing the earth's oceans, seas, and other bodies of water, to shield you from negativity, for protection (especially of women and children), and to heal emotional trauma (especially those experiences dealing with physical or verbal abuse).

MOQUI MARBLES: (Also known as Mochi Marbles or Maqui Marbles) Use at the 1st Chakra (Root Chakra) or at the 6th Chakra (3rd Eye/Brow Chakra) for Shamanic journeying, to facilitate a connection with nature, for grounding, for protection, or balance of male and female energies, to balance the yin and yang aspects of your personality, to enhance esoteric knowledge of occult topics, and to enhance mystical experiences.

MORGANITE: (Also known as Pink Beryl) Use at the 2nd Chakra (Sacral Chakra) or at the 4th Chakra (Heart Chakra) to facilitate emotional stability, to enhance feelings of love and protection, to increase self-love, to re-open your heart chakra after heartbreak or great loss, and to aid your feeling of comfort with himself or herself without the influence of the ego-self.

-N-

NEPHRITE, GREEN: (Also known as Green Nephrite Jade) Use at the 4th Chakra (Heart Chakra) to bring wealth and prosperity, to facilitate a connection with nature, for healing, to enhance your knowledge of plants and the plant kingdom (especially in skills such as herbalism), to encourage good health, and to promote good luck.

NUUMMITE: Use at the 7th Chakra (Crown Chakra) for astral projection, to shield your energy body from psychic attack, to open you up to new ideas, to aid in removing old patterns and behaviors, to aid you in overcoming your self-limiting beliefs, to stimulate intuition & psychic awareness, to balance and align body, mind, and spirit, to connect you with beings from the fairy realm, to aid you in seeing your inner beauty, and to enhance divination practices.

-O-

OBSIDIAN, BLACK: Use at the 1st Chakra (Root Chakra) for protection, to reveal the truth in any situation, to expose areas of you that need growth and development, to facilitate past life ascension and regression, to block negative energies from entering your auric field, for grounding, to shield you from electromagnetic pollution, to banish negative energy, to bring peace and calming, to encourage living in a virtuous manner, to encourage personal growth, to increase courage, to facilitate compassion, to reduce arthritis pain, to detoxify the physical body, to maintain proper circulation, for use in scrying divination, to balance the mind, body, and spirit, to aid in acceptance of your weaknesses and to begin to heal and correct them, to address issues of control and power struggles, for use in shamanic ceremonies and rituals, and to remove negative thought patterns and conditioning.

OBSIDIAN, COLORLESS: (Also known as Lake County Diamonds) Use at the 6th Chakra (3rd Eye/Brow Chakra) or at the 7th Chakra (Crown Chakra) to enhance psychic awareness and intuition, for promoting mental clarity (especially during times of great stress), to enhance the flow of energy during Reiki and other types of energy healing, and to dissolve energy blockages.

OBSIDIAN, GOLD SHEEN: Use at the 6th Chakra (3rd Eye/Brow Chakra) or at the 7th Chakra (Crown Chakra) to stimulate your clairvoyant abilities (psychic sight), to connect you with your ancestors for guidance, to heal problems associated with the brain or nervous system (including stroke and aneurysm), for scrying divination, and to use during shamanic journeying.

OBSIDIAN, MAHOGANY: Use at the 1st Chakra (Root Chakra) to enhance your vitality and zest for life, to instill level-headedness in times of chaos and turmoil, to help you find balance between the spiritual and physical realms, for protection, to connect you with the energies of the Goddess Pele, and to establish a lasting connection with mother earth.

OBSIDIAN, PEACOCK: (Also known as Velvet Obsidian) Use at the 1st Chakra (Root Chakra), 6th Chakra (3rd Eye/Brow Chakra), or 7th Chakra (Crown Chakra) to stimulate intuition and psychic awareness, to facilitate communication with higher beings, for shamanic journeying or soul journeying, to facilitate astral travel of any kind, and to access the dream consciousness while in the waking state.

OBSIDIAN, RAINBOW SHEEN: Use at the 1st Chakra (Root Chakra), 6th Chakra (3rd Eye/Brow Chakra), or at the 7th Chakra (Crown Chakra) for emotional healing, to guide soul journeying or shamanic journeying, and to promote self-realization. Use at any chakra for cleansing, balancing, and alignment.

OBSIDIAN, SNOWFLAKE: (Also known as Phenocryst-Included Black Obsidian or as Flowering Obsidian) Obsidian or as Flowering Obsidian) Use at the 1st Chakra (Root Chakra) for protection, to reveal the truth in any situation, to expose areas of you that need growth and development, to facilitate past life ascension and regression, to block negative energies from entering your auric field, for grounding, to shield you from electromagnetic pollution, to banish negative energy, to bring peace and calming, to encourage living in a virtuous manner, to encourage personal growth, to instill determination, to facilitate communication with your guides and angels, to increase courage, to stimulate intuition, to facilitate compassion, to reduce arthritis pain, to detoxify the physical body, to maintain proper circulation, to balance mind, body, and spirit, to encourage independence, and to improve circulation.

OKENITE: (Also known as "Fuzzy Rock") Use at the 7th Chakra (Crown Chakra) for purification, to uplift you spiritually, to enhance a connection with your higher self, to promote divine guidance, to help you learn about tenderness, to bring the light into even the darkest situations, to aid you in seeing the good in all things, and to remove the ego and let the spirit shine.

ONYX, BLACK: (Also known as Black Chalcedony) Use at the 1st Chakra (Root Chakra) to enhance clear focus, to amplify your intention, to promote Divine order, to encourage sensibility, for protection and shielding from negative energies, and for grounding.

OPAL, ANDEAN BLUE (COMMON): Use at the 4th Chakra (Heart Chakra) or at the 5th Chakra (Throat Chakra) for promoting compassionate attitudes, to encourage heart-based speech and actions, for enhancing Shamanic work, to center the self, to quiet the ego mind, and for peace and tranquility.

OPAL, ANDEAN PINK (COMMON): (Also known as Andes' Pink Opal or as Peruvian Pink Opal) Use at the 4th Chakra (Heart Chakra) to instill love and compassion in the user, to enhance prayers and intentions for the good of all beings, to help heal afflictions of the heart, to cool fiery tensions caused by family disagreements (especially those stemming from sibling rivalry), to encourage forgiveness, to instill a feeling of nurturing and tenderness toward all beings, for healing heart trauma (physical or emotional), to protect the heart chakra, to add a new spark to old relationships, to provide comfort for those who are terminally ill, to guide you down your life path, and to promote emotional stability and security.

OPAL, ANDEAN PINK DENDRITIC (COMMON): (Also known as Pink Dendritic Peruvian Opal) Use at the 1st Chakra (Root Chakra) or at the 4th Chakra (Heart Chakra) to expand the energies of the heart chakra throughout your entire physical and energetic bodies, to anchor the energies of the heart chakra in your everyday life so that he or she may remember to treat all beings with love, kindness, and compassion, to extinguish feelings of anger and replace them with peace and understanding, and to aid you in recognizing the oneness of all beings.

OPAL, BOULDER (PRECIOUS): Use at the 5th Chakra (Throat Chakra) or at the 6th Chakra (3rd Eye/Brow Chakra) to balance and align all chakras, to restore you to optimum health after times of stress or negativity, to allow you to remain positive and optimistic until your hopes, dreams, and wishes have been fulfilled, to promote harmony in friendships and partnerships, and to allow you to see auras.

OPAL, FIRE (PRECIOUS): (Also known as Cherry Opal) Use at the 1st Chakra (Root Chakra), 2nd Chakra (Sacral Chakra), 6th Chakra (3rd Eye/Brow Chakra), or at the 7th Chakra (Crown Chakra) to stimulate vitality and passion for life, to enhance connection to the fire element, to instill creative inspiration, for treating depression or apathy, to enhance telepathic communication, to stimulate your psychic abilities, and to promote spiritual ascension.

OPAL, HYALINE (COMMON): (Also known as Hyalite) Use at the 6th Chakra (3rd Eye/Brow Chakra) or at the 7th Chakra (Crown Chakra) to raise your energetic vibrations, for spiritual ascension, to remove feelings of jealousy or anger, to connect you with your inner child, and to combine and balance the energies of the air and water elements within the body.

OPAL, WHITE (COMMON): Use at the 6th Chakra (3rd Eye Chakra) to promote healthy sleep patterns, for sweet dreams, to remove fear and anxiety, to connect you with the water element, to connect with the energy of the Goddess Yemaya, and for inner peace.

ORPIMENT: Use at the 2nd Chakra (Sacral Chakra) to use treatment of cancer or tumorous growths. PLEASE NOTE: Orpiment contains Arsenic, so please wash your hands thoroughly after handling.

-P-

PAPAGOITE: Use at the 5th Chakra (Throat Chakra) to heal other energy healers, to aid you in manifesting abundance, to instill an "attitude of gratitude," to remove any energetic blockages from the etheric body, to liberate you spiritually, to aid you in seeing the truth, to work through feelings of grief, to aid in understanding and respecting the sacredness of all things and the oneness that connects them, to enhance the power of crystal healing, to aid you in understanding crystal energies more fully, and to facilitate the remembering of your past life memories.

PEARL, WHITE: Use at the 6th Chakra (3rd Eye/Brow Chakra) or at the 7th Chakra (Crown Chakra) to promote cooperation, to provide a connection with Goddess energy, to stimulate a nurturing attitude, and to promote peace.

PERIDOT: (Also known as Olivine) Use at the 4th Chakra (Heart Chakra) for protection, to disintegrate negative energy, for healing the body, mind, and spirit, to manifest physical and spiritual abundance, and to increase luck.

PETALITE: Use at the 5th Chakra (Throat Chakra) or at the 7th Chakra (Crown Chakra) to establish a connection with your spirit guides, guardian angels, or totem animals, for purification, to shield the user with white light when in negative energy environments, for protection (especially of children or animals), to help heal the spirit, to remind you of your divine nature, for use with babies and children (or after a near-death experience) to ease the transition from the other side into the physical world, and to be a constant reminder of the light and of your spirit when you are distracted by your ego-self.

PIETERSITE, BLUE: Use at the 5th Chakra (Throat Chakra) or 6th Chakra (3rd Eye/Brow Chakra) for stimulating intuition and psychic ability, to facilitate astral travel, for spiritual ascension, to enhance guidance and visions received during meditation, and to aid in developing lucid dreaming skills.

PIETERSITE, RED: Use at the 1st Chakra (Root Chakra), 2nd Chakra (Sacral Chakra/Solar Plexus Chakra), or at the 6th Chakra (3rd Eye/Brow Chakra) to increase vitality, to promote healthy functioning of the organs, to stimulate creativity and artistic vision, to aid in increasing strength and flexibility of the physical body, to instill will-power and determination, and to protect you from complications during childbirth.

PRASIOLITE: (Also known as Green Amethyst, Praseolite, or as Amegreen) Use at the 4th Chakra (Heart Chakra), 6th Chakra (3rd Eye/Brow Chakra), or 7th Chakra (Crown Chakra) to facilitate a connection to the inner self, to establish a connection with nature and with nature spirits, to heal the mind, body, and spirit, to instill compassion and empathy, and for balancing the chakras.

PREHNITE: Use at the 4th Chakra (Heart Chakra) to establish a connection with Earth energies and with nature, to promote feelings of peace, to aid in spiritual guidance, to increase happiness, to aid in dematerialization and the letting go of worldly goods, to promote a feeling of spiritual fulfillment, to aid in communication with nature spirits such as faeries, sprites, gnomes, and elves, for earth healing, to stimulate compassion and empathy, to guide you down your life path, and for spiritual ascension.

PRESELI BLUE STONE: (Also known as Stonehenge Rock or as Stonehenge Stone) Use at the 6th Chakra (3rd Eye/Brow Chakra) or at the 7th Chakra (Crown Chakra) to promote altered states of consciousness, to connect with extra-terrestrials, to enhance ritual and ceremony, and to connect you with the energy vortex at the Stonehenge site.

PROPHECY STONE: (Also known as Hematite Pseudomorph after Marcasite) Use at the 6th Chakra (3rd Eye/Brow Chakra) to enhance your natural channeling abilities, to aid you in developing your intuition and psychic awareness, to get in touch with ancient wisdom and knowledge, and to access information from the Akashic Records.

PSILOMELANE: Use at the 1st Chakra (Root Chakra) or at the 6th Chakra (3rd Eye/Brow Chakra) to strengthen the etheric cord that connects the energy bodies to the physical body, to dissolve blockages in the energy field, to overcome self-limiting beliefs, to banish outworn patterns and systems, and to transmute negative thoughts into positive thoughts).

PYRITE: (Also known as Fool's Gold, as Inca's Gold, or as Inca's Mirror) Use at the 3rd (Solar Plexus Chakra) for an increase in vitality, to conquer vices, to build confidence, for protection, to block electromagnetic pollution, to ward off infection, to aid in business endeavors, to promote group cooperation, to remove worries, to balance the conscious and unconscious minds, to banish depression, to increase vitality, to balance the ethereal body, for grounding, to encourage creativity, to aid in focus and concentration, to help manifest abundance and prosperity, and to treat infertility.

PYRITE, ISIS & OSIRIS: Use at the 3rd Chakra (Solar Plexus Chakra) to balance male and female energies and to correct other types of energetic imbalances, to strengthen your personal power without using the ego, to connect you with your spirit guides (especially those stemming from the Egyptian pantheon), to bring the healing energies of the sun and moon into the body, to enhance relationships between partners, and for facilitating astral travel and dream healing.

PYRITE SUN: (Also known as a Pyrite Sand-Dollar) Use at the 3rdChakra to bring the warmth and light of the sun into the etheric bodies, to radiate confidence and will-power to all aspects of the self, to promote joy and happiness, and to aid you in manifesting abundance.

PYROMORPHITE: Use at the 1st Chakra (Root Chakra), 3rd Chakra (Solar Plexus Chakra), or at the 4th Chakra (Heart Chakra) to instill a sense of child-like wonder in adults, to allow you to see beings from the fairy realm, to aid in creating a relationship with and appreciation for nature (down to the tiniest of beings), to aid you in walking a simple path in life, and for helping you to find balance in life between the natural world and the modern world (and to aid you in eventually realizing the oneness of these "separate" things).

-Q-

QUANTUM QUATTRO SILICA: This very high energy stone is a combination of Chrysocolla, Malachite, Dioptase, and Shattuckite in a matrix of Smoky Quartz. I can be used at any chakra to bring balance to the particular energy center. It connects the user with direct access to the healing energy of the Earth and is strongly aligned with Goddess energy. Since this stone is comprised of five other minerals, it contains the energy of each of those five as well.

QUARTZ, AJOITE-INCLUDED: Use between the 4th Chakra (Heart Chakra) and the 5th Chakra (Throat Chakra), to enhance communication (allowing the user to speak form the heart), to facilitate a connection with your spirit guides or guardian angels, to enhance meditation, for spiritual ascension, to aid you in working through karmic obstacles, to enhance knowledge gained form shamanic journeying, and for emotional balance and stability.

QUARTZ, AMETHYST AURA: (Also known as Lavender Aura Quartz) Use at the 6th Chakra (3rd Eye/Brow Chakra) or at the 7th Chakra (Crown Chakra) to bring about feelings of spiritual wholeness, to instill happiness and joy, to enhance Zen states and meditation practices, to give you a sense of child-like wonder, and to connect you with nature spirits and beings of the Faery Realm.

QUARTZ, ANGEL AURA: (Also known as Opal Aura Quartz or as Pearl Aura Quartz) Use at the 4th Chakra (Heart Chakra) or 7th Chakra (Crown Chakra) to open you to divine knowledge, to stimulate deep spiritual experiences, to promote successful meditation, to aid in establishing a connection to your angels or guides, to bring love and light into any situation, to promote feelings of safety and security, to enhance Lovingkindness, to facilitate peace and calming, to mend broken relationships, to enhance forgiveness on you or of others, and to enhance compassionate attitudes.

QUARTZ, ANGEL ROSE: Use at the 4th Chakra (Heart Chakra) or at the 7th Chakra (Crown Chakra) to bring angelic energies into the heart, to allow you to see the divine nature in all other beings and to truly experience the oneness of all, and for protection of children and animals.

QUARTZ, APPLE AURA: (Also known as Emerald Aura Quartz) Use at the 3rd Chakra (Solar Plexus Chakra) or at the 4th Chakra (Heart Chakra) to purify the energy body, to balance and align all chakras, to relieve digestive problems or upset stomach, to bring about necessary change and to break old patterns or belief systems, to instill courage, and to help you to appreciate the beauty in life's everyday happenings.

QUARTZ, AQUA AURA: Use at the 5th Chakra (Throat Chakra) or 6th Chakra (3rd Eye/Brow Chakra) for opening you to psychic insight, to strengthen the heart chakra energies, to connect the heart chakra with the throat chakra (allowing you to speak your inner truth), to help you to grow and evolve as a spiritual being, to connect you to your spirit guides, for astral travel, and to facilitate shamanic journeying.

QUARTZ, BLUE TARA: (Also known as Olenite-Included Quartz, as Indicolite-Included Quartz, as Indigolite-Included Quartz, or as Blue Tourmaline-Included Quartz) Use at the 5th Chakra (Throat Chakra) or at the 6th Chakra (3rd Eye/Brow Chakra) to help heal the eyes, to facilitate communication with your spirit guides, to promote Buddha-like attitudes, to connect you with the water element, to promote change, to facilitate a connection with the energy of the spiritual centers of Tibet, to connect you with your totem animal (especially with the wolf), for protection (especially of women and children), and to banish anger and replace it with compassion.

QUARTZ, CELADONITE PHANTOM: Use at the 4th Chakra (Heart Chakra) Use at the heart chakra or over sensitive organs when performing psychic surgery or deeply penetrating energy work. This stone has a very gentle energy and is one of the few stones that may be used in these delicate areas of the body.

QUARTZ, CHAMPAGNE AURA: Use at the 3rd Chakra (Solar Plexus Chakra) or at the 7th Chakra (Crown Chakra) to bring divine energy into the body for healing the physical, emotional, or spiritual aspects of the self, to aid in spiritual ascension, to connect you with the divine for channeling information, to open you to new experiences (so that they may not need be repeated in a future lifetime), and to stimulate your conscious awareness.

QUARTZ, CHLORITE-INCLUDED: Use at the 1st Chakra (Root Chakra) or at the 4th Chakra (Heart Chakra) for stimulating the metabolism and helping you to lose weight, to aid in the absorption of nutrients and antioxidants, to promote general physical healing, to rehabilitate strained or injured muscles, and to connect you with nature and with mother earth herself.

QUARTZ, COBALT AURA: (Also known as Royal Aura Quartz, Steel Blue Aura Quartz, or as Azure Aura Quartz)) Use at the 6th Chakra (3rd Eye/Brow Chakra) to dissipate feelings of anger, to aid in developing a state of non-attachment, to aid in enhancing meditative states, to facilitate a connection with the emotional body, and to provide the opportunity to learn from the water element.

QUARTZ, COLORLESS: (Also known as Rock Crystal) Clear Quartz crystals can be used at any chakra and are by far the most powerful and energizing crystals of all. Quartz is a powerful healer and purifying cleanser of the physical and ethereal body. Quartz crystals amplify your own energies and intentions and thus are ideal for any kind of spiritual work.

QUARTZ, COPPER AURA: Use at the 1st Chakra (Root Chakra) or at the 2nd Chakra (Sacral Chakra) for grounding, to relieve pain caused by inflammation, to allow you to see your shadow side in order aid in self-growth and self-evolution, to aid in healing past-life trauma, to balance the emotions, and to enhance vitality.

QUARTZ, DIAMANTINA: Use at any chakra to balance and align the energy body, to bring in healing energy form the universe to correct and parts of the body in which dis-ease has manifested, and to project universal healing light into the universe for the highest good of all beings.

QUARTZ, DREAM: (Also known as Epidote-Included Quartz) – Use at the 6th Chakra (3rd Eye/Brow Chakra) to aid in dream healing, to facilitate astral travel, to enhance lucid dreaming practices, to help heal ailing house plants, and to help bring calming vibrations to distraught indigo children.

QUARTZ, EDENITE-INCLUDED: Use at the 4th Chakra (Heart Chakra) to balance the masculine and feminine energies of the user, to help couples with working out relationship problems, to aid in banishing temptation, to bring order out of chaos, to aid you in returning to your roots, and for channeling (especially when communicating with your ancestors).

QUARTZ, ELECTRIC BLUE AURA: Use at the 5th Chakra (Throat Chakra) to enhance communication with your guardian angels, spirit guides, totem animals, ascended masters, or with your higher self; to promote spiritual ascension; to instill peace and calming; to relieve anxiety; to remove negativity from the energy body; and to reduce stress caused by putting pressure on you.

QUARTZ, FADEN: (Also known as Thread Quartz or as Tube Quartz) Use at the 2nd Chakra (Sacral Chakra), at the 6th Chakra (3rd Eye/Brow Chakra) or at the 7th Chakra (Crown Chakra) to enhance psychic energy, to gain spiritual insight, to enhance meditation, and to aid in facilitating a connection to and communication with your inner self and with your higher self. You may also align the Faden line with the spine to heal and balance the energy of your chakras and aura. Align the Faden line between two people to enhance telepathy and the ability to sense each other's energy.

QUARTZ, FERTILITY: Use at the 1st Chakra (Root Chakra) or at the 2nd Chakra (Sacral Chakra) to promote male and female fertility, to aid you in carrying a pregnancy to term, to increase your prosperity and abundance, to stimulate creative energies, and to balance your masculine and feminine energies.

QUARTZ, FIRE: (Also known as Harlequin Quartz) Use at the 1st Chakra (Root Chakra) or at the

2nd Chakra (Sacral Chakra) to enhance vitality, to promote healthy and balanced sexual energy, to connect you with the energy of the fire element, to burn away feelings of shame or guilt by promoting self-forgiveness, to help heal past life trauma by putting an end to repeating detrimental behavioral patterns, and to promote confidence and self-reliance (by banishing co-dependent habits and behaviors).

QUARTZ, FLUORITE-INCLUDED PURPLE: (Also known as Blue Joy Quartz or as Purple Fluor Spar Included Quartz) Use at the 7th Chakra (Crown Chakra) to connect you with the energies of the air element, to help you overcome mental obstacles by providing reassurance and allowing you to see that *there are no impossibilities*, to help you eliminate addictive behavioral patterns, to promote clarity of mind, and to aid in slowing memory loss.

QUARTZ, GIRASOL: (Also known as Girasol or as Opalized Quartz) Use at the 6th Chakra (3rd Eye/Brow Chakra) or at the 7th Chakra (Crown Chakra) as a way to stay connected with the inner self during times of turmoil and great change, to aid in the ascension process, to aid in discerning unclear or clouded intuitive messages, to facilitate a connection to the angelic realm, to aid you in seeing the hidden meaning behind a situation, to aid in karmic upliftment, to safely protect you with universal white light energy, to allow you to live your life for you (but in an ego-less manner), for spiritual awakening, for healing the body, mind, and spirit, by way of divine energy, and to aid you in channeling.

QUARTZ, GOLDEN HEALER: Use at the 3rd Chakra (Solar Plexus Chakra) or at the 7th Chakra (Crown Chakra) to enhance the flow of energy during healing work of any kind, to aid a healer or energy worker to stay grounded while giving healing, to open a healer to Universal Source energy for the good of his/her client, and to enhance inner strength and personal power.

QUARTZ, GOLDEN MAYANITE: Use at the 6th Chakra (3rd Eye Chakra) or at the 7th Chakra (Crown Chakra) to connect with Divine energy, for purifying the lightbody, to enhance your natural healing skills, to connect with the energy of crystal skulls (and to better channel/access their knowledge and wisdom), to enhance channeling, and to bring the light of the Divine into your life (furthering your path as a Lightworker)

QUARTZ, HEMATITE-INCLUDED: Use at the 1st Chakra (Root Chakra) to cleanse and purify the blood and internal organs, to stimulate vitality, for protection, to relieve pain associated with strained muscles or damaged ligaments or tendons, to instill courage and bravery, and for guidance on your career path.

QUARTZ, HEMATITE-INCLUDED RED PHANTOM: Use at the 1st Chakra (Root Chakra) for encouraging deeper states of meditation, for grounding, to remove negativity from your thinking or to remove negative energy from the aura, for vitality, and to enhance intuitive wisdom.

QUARTZ, HERKIMER DIAMOND: (Also known as Herkimer Diamond) Use at the 6th Chakra (3rd Eye/Brow Chakra) or 7th Chakra (Crown Chakra) to facilitate astral travel, to promote lucid dreaming, to fully access the dream consciousness while in the waking state, for aid in balancing and aligning the chakra system, and to enhance clarity of thought. Herkimer Diamond Quartz is a good companion stone for Moldavite. When used together, the stones will enhance each other's qualities.

QUARTZ, HOLLANDITE: (Also known as Spider Quartz or as Star Quartz) Use at the 7th Chakra (Crown Chakra) to enhance your connection to the Divine, to open your crown chakra to new spiritual ideals, to awaken your higher self, to enhance meditation, and to balance your physical, mental, and spiritual aspects.

QUARTZ, KIWI AURA: Use at the 4th Chakra (Heart Chakra) or at the 5th Chakra (Throat Chakra) to instill a deep appreciation for nature, to connect you with nature spirits and beings of the Fairy Realm, to heal blockages caused by emotional trauma, to instill courage and bravery in the user, to promote feelings of comfort and safety (especially when in strange places), and to encourage self-love and forgiveness.

QUARTZ, LAVENDER ROSE: Use at the 4th Chakra (Heart Chakra) or at the 7th Chakra (Crown Chakra) for allowing you to realize that all is full of love. This stone harmonizes the energies of Rose Quartz and Amethyst.

QUARTZ, LEMURIAN STAR SEED: (Also known as Lemurian Seed Quartz or as Lemurian Quartz) Use at the 6th Chakra (3rd Eye/Brow Chakra) or 7th Chakra (Crown Chakra) for drawing in Universal energy and gridding it here on the Earth, to connect you to the ancient civilization of Lemuria (also known as Mu) and the esoteric wisdom of this culture, to communicate the idea of oneness and love to all other crystals on the planet, and to transmit energy from the stars to the Earth. Lemurian Seed Crystals come from a specific mine in Brazil that is thought to be located on the site of the ancient Lemurian society. They are typically very clear and have 6 sides (which alternate between smooth and horizontally striated/grooved sides. These crystals are from a special mine in Brazil and are said to have been placed there for safe-keeping by the Lemurians until such a time as they were needed on earth. It is said that coded/programmed information has been stored on their striated surfaces and can be accessed by some Lightworkers via meditation and physical interaction with the stones.

QUARTZ, LEMURIAN STAR SEED PINK: (Also known as Pink Lemurian Seed Quartz or as Pink Lemurian Quartz) Use at the 4th Chakra (Heart Chakra) or at the 7th Chakra (Crown Chakra) to bring Universal healing energy into the physical and energetic bodies, to open chakras that have closed due to emotional trauma and to bring peace and calming.

QUARTZ, LITHIUM-INCLUDED: (Also known as Lithium Phantom Quartz) Use at the 4th Chakra (Heart Chakra) or at the 6th Chakra (3rd Eye/Brow

Chakra) to banish depression, to balance the hemispheres of the brain, to promote tranquility and peace in the user, to dispel anxiety, and to promote emotional healing (especially related to trauma or grief).

QUARTZ, MELON AURA: (Also known as Tangerine Aura Quartz, Imperial Gold Aura Quartz, Dreamcicle Aura Quartz, or as Orange Mist Aura Quartz) Use at the 2nd Chakra (Sacral Chakra), 3rd Chakra (Solar Plexus Chakra), or at the 4th Chakra (Heart Chakra) to stimulate compassion, to promote forgiveness (of you and of others), to heal the emotional body, to repair damaged relationships between parents and children, and to instill happiness and joy.

QUARTZ, METAMORPHOSIS™: Use at any chakra to bring about necessary change, to heal imbalances in the energy body, to connect with the emotions and with the water element, to increase your knowledge is the practical application of crystals for healing, and for transformation of you for the highest good of all beings.

QUARTZ, MILKY: (Also known as White Quartz, Snow Quartz, or as Quartzite) Use at the 5th Chakra (Throat Chakra) or at the 7th Chakra (Crown Chakra) to stimulate creativity, to overcome blocks in your intuition, to shield the psychic body, to bring inner peace and tranquility, to aid in deepening your meditation practice, for keeping you grounded during astral travel, and for use during prayer or worship.

QUARTZ, MILLENNIUM ORANGE: (Also known as a Carnelian nodule) Use at the 3rd Chakra (Solar Plexus Chakra) to promote shifts in consciousness (personal and planetary), for grounding, to ease the physical symptoms that can accompany energetic shifts, and for healing and repairing the mental body.

QUARTZ, NIRVANA PINK: (Also known as Pink Ice Quartz, Pink Himalayan Quartz, or as Pink Glacial Quartz) Use at the 4th Chakra (Heart Chakra), 6th Chakra (3rd Eye/Brow Chakra), or at the 7th Chakra (Crown Chakra) to open the heart chakra, for protection (especially of mothers and children), to aid in healing disorders of the heart, to regulate circulation and blood pressure, to promote love and compassion for the earth and all her children, for aiding in earth healing work and to encourage proper care of the earth, to enhance Lovingkindness meditation, to instill a sense of the importance of eco-friendly practices, for promoting spiritual ascension, to enhance the love between partners, and to promote peace and harmony.

QUARTZ, NIRVANA WHITE: (Also known as White Ice Quartz, White Himalayan Quartz, or as White Glacial Quartz) Use at the 4th Chakra (Heart Chakra), 6th Chakra (3rd Eye/Brow Chakra), or at the 7th Chakra (Crown Chakra) to raise your energetic vibration during healing and meditation work, to promote astral travel, to enhance the effects of healing work, to connect you with the knowledge of the ancient peoples of the earth, and to promote cellular repair and DNA level healing within the body.

QUARTZ, OURO VERDE: (Also known as Green-Gold Quartz or as Gold-Green Quartz) Use at the 1st Chakra (Root Chakra), 3rd Chakra (Solar Plexus Chakra), or at the 7th Chakra (Crown Chakra) to bring spiritual illumination, to remove obstacles on your path to enlightenment, to enhance your inner knowing and self-confidence, to lay your path before you, to remind you of your soul contract or karmic debts while on the Earth plane, and to help facilitate astral travel for the purposes of healing or gathering information.

QUARTZ, PAPAYA: Use at the 2nd Chakra (Sacral Chakra) or at the 3rd Chakra (Solar Plexus Chakra) to aid in digestion, to relieve an upset stomach, to aid in the absorption on nutrients form your food, to aid your body in using natural antioxidants (especially for cancer prevention), to reduce fever, to aid you in stilling the mind during meditation, and to facilitate healthy weight loss.

QUARTZ, PECOS DIAMOND: (Also known as Pecos Valley Diamond, Pecos Valley Diamond Quartz, or as Pecos Quartz) Use at the 1st Chakra (Root Chakra), 2nd Chakra (Sacral Chakra), 6th Chakra (3rd Eye/Brow Chakra), or at the 7th Chakra (Crown Chakra) for stimulating creativity, to enhance your intuitive guidance, to aid in the spiritual ascension process, to stimulate sexual energy, to balance the emotional bodies, and to promote feelings of happiness and joy.

QUARTZ, RAINBOW AURA: (Also known as Flame Aura Quartz) Use at the 1st Chakra (Root

Chakra/Base Chakra), 6th Chakra (3rd Eye/Brow Chakra), or 7th Chakra (Crown Chakra) to stimulate a connection with the divine, to enhance psychic insight, to facilitate a spiritual connection with nature, to aid in seeing and reading auras, to promote lucid dreaming and dream recall, and for promoting positive self-reflection.

QUARTZ, ROSE: (Also known as Anacona Ruby) Use at the 4th Chakra (Heart Chakra) for promoting unconditional love, peace, and compassion, to inspire self-love, to promote an attitude of Lovingkindness, for calming after traumatic events, to instill tenderness, to add spark to a romance, to ease mid-life crisis, to soothe a broken heart, for emotional balance, to encourage friendship, to ease the grieving process, to promote forgiveness, trust, and understanding, to help with healing lungs, to increase fertility, and to treat a poor complexion.

QUARTZ, ROSE AURA: (Also known as Raspberry Aura Quartz) Use at the 4th Chakra (Heart Chakra) to instill a sense of Lovingkindess; to help heal emotional trauma; to aid in enhancing forgiveness; to aid in recovering from any type of abuse on a physical, mental, emotional, and spiritual level; and to help you find a tactful way to communicate in difficult situations.

QUARTZ, ROSE ELESTIAL: (Also known as Rose Skeletal Quartz or as Rose Jacare Quartz) Use at the 4th Chakra (Heart Chakra) to facilitate a connection between you and loved ones on the other side, for protection during astral travel, to connect you with beings from the angelic realms, to aid in emotional healing, to promote feelings of safety and security, to balance the body, mind, and spirit, to aid in the spiritual ascension process, to aid you in the realization that all is full of love, and to aid in healing meditations of all kinds.

QUARTZ, RUBY AURA: Use at the 1st Chakra (Root Chakra) to instill vitality, to aid the body in detoxing, for motivation, to help warm the physical body (especially when you have symptoms of the flu such as chills), to aid in moving the Kundalini energy throughout the body (either rising or returning to the resting state), and to promote balanced circulation in the body.

QUARTZ, RUTILATED ANGEL: Use at the 5th Chakra (Throat Chakra), 6th Chakra (3rd Eye/Brow Chakra), or 7th Chakra (Crown Chakra) to facilitate contact with the angelic realm and to enhance communication with angelic beings, to facilitate the transfer of vibrational healing energies, to remove barriers interfering with spiritual growth, to open you to the Divine energy of the Universe, to heal and repair the aura, to promote spiritual ascension, to bring the light of the divine into your physical body on earth, to enhance your connection with your guardian angels and to enhance the protection that they provide.

QUARTZ, RUTILATED GOLDEN: (Also known as Golden Angel Hair Quartz or as Golden Venus Hair Quartz) Use at the 3rd Chakra (Solar Plexus Chakra) or at the 7th Chakra (Crown Chakra) for increasing vitality, to facilitate the transfer of vibrational healing energies, to balance body, mind, and spirit, to cleanse the aura, to manifest spiritual abundance, to facilitate astral travel, scrying divination, and channeling sessions, to remove barriers interfering with spiritual growth, to open you to the Divine energy of the Universe, for protection from negative energy vibrations, to aid in past life ascension and regression, to aid in acceptance of the soul's current life purpose and lessons, to heal the spirit, to facilitate positive change, to encourage forgiveness and compassion, to remove depression, to heal and repair the aura, to promote spiritual ascension, to increase fertility, to restore energy to the physical body, to balance the thyroid, and to promote proper posture.

QUARTZ, RUTILATED RED: (Also known as Red Venus Hair Quartz or as Red Angel Hair Quartz) Use at the 3rd Chakra (Solar Plexus Chakra) or at the 7th Chakra (Crown Chakra) for increasing vitality, to facilitate the transfer of vibrational healing energies, to balance body, mind, and spirit, to cleanse the aura, to manifest spiritual abundance, to facilitate astral travel, scrying divination, and channeling sessions, to remove barriers interfering with spiritual growth, to open you to the Divine energy of the Universe, for protection from negative energy vibrations, to aid in past life ascension and regression, to aid in acceptance of the soul's current life purpose and lessons, to heal the spirit, to facilitate positive change, to encourage forgiveness and compassion, to remove depression, to heal and repair the aura, to promote spiritual ascension, to increase fertility, to restore energy to the physical body, to balance the thyroid, and to promote proper posture.

QUARTZ, RUTILATED SILVER: (Also known as Silver Angel Hair Quartz or as Silver Venus Hair Quartz) Use at the 3rd Chakra (Solar Plexus Chakra) or at the 7th Chakra (Crown Chakra) for increasing vitality, to facilitate the transfer of vibrational healing energies, to balance body, mind, and spirit, to cleanse the aura, to manifest spiritual abundance, to facilitate astral travel, scrying divination, and channeling sessions, to remove barriers interfering with spiritual growth, to open you to the Divine energy of the Universe, for protection from negative energy vibrations, to aid in past life ascension and regression, to aid in acceptance of the soul's current life purpose and lessons, to heal the spirit, to facilitate positive change, to encourage forgiveness and compassion, to remove depression, to heal and repair the aura, to promote spiritual ascension, to increase fertility, to restore energy to the physical body, to balance the thyroid, and to promote proper posture.

QUARTZ, SATYALOKA: (Also known as Satyaloka Monastery Quartz) Use at the 7th Chakra (Crown Chakra) for spiritual ascension, to raise the vibration of the physical body to match the vibration of the spiritual body, to balance and align the chakra centers, to repair tears or holes in the auric field, to activate the light body, to enhance meditation (especially when placed over the 3rd Eye), and to remove attachments to the physical plane.

QUARTZ, SERIPHOS: (Also known as African Jade, Prase, Prasem, Hedenbergite-Included Quartz, Seraphos Quartz, Seraphos Green Quartz, Seriphos Green Quartz, Seraphos, or as Seriphos) Use at the 4th Chakra (Heart Chakra) for aiding in the realization that all is full of love, to aid you to feel comfortable in your physical body here on Earth, to enhance your connection with nature and with the Earth, to promote a sense of ego-less pride, to enhance intuitive wisdom, to aid in manifesting prosperity and abundance, to heal disorders of the eyes, to heal physical and emotional ailments of the heart, and to promote peace and calming.

QUARTZ, SHAMANIC DREAM: (Also known as Lodolite-Included Quartz or as Shamanic Dream Stones) Use at the 1st Chakra (Root Chakra) or at the 6th Chakra (3rd Eye/Brow Chakra) to aid in spiritual shamanic journeying, to enhance your conscious awareness, to deepen states of meditation, to promote meaningful astral travel, to induce ecstatic states of existence (as during spiritual experiences, vision quests, etc.), to heighten your intuition and psychic powers, and to protect the brujo/bruja during spiritual work. Shamanic Dream Quartz has the ability to stimulate amazing Shamanic journeys while, later, has the ability to pull the astral body back down to the earth plane.

QUARTZ, SMOKY: (Also known as Smokey Quartz) Use at the 1st Chakra (Root Chakra) for grounding, protection from negative energy, to increase energy during meditation, to encourage environmental concern and ecological consciousness, to relieve stress and promote peace and calming, to block electromagnetic pollution, to aid in detoxifying the physical body, to remove fear, to enhance passion, to dispel bad dreams, to use in scrying divination to promote insight, to stimulate concentration, to promote communication, to aid in stilling the mind for successful meditation, for use with people undergoing chemotherapy, to aid in manifesting, to assist you in managing detailed projects, to relieve physical pain, to treat problems associated with the lower half of the physical body, to remove headache pain, and to aid in the assimilation of vitamins and minerals.

QUARTZ, SMOKY-CITRINE: Use at the 2nd Chakra (Sacral Chakra) to provide relief from symptoms of intestinal disorders, to aid you in putting down new roots after times of turmoil or change, to help you to step outside of the self to see problems caused by your ego consciousness, to unite the 1st Chakra energies with the 7th Chakra energies in order to bring universal spiritual energy into your day-to-day life, and to instill a sense of gratitude for what you already have in life (to banish desire for material things).

QUARTZ, SPIRIT: (Also known as Fairy Quartz, as Faery Quartz, as Pineapple Quartz, or as Cactus Quartz) Use at the 3rd Chakra (Solar Plexus Chakra), 6th Chakra (3rd Eye/Brow Chakra), or at the 7th Chakra (Crown Chakra) to facilitate a connection with your Spirit Guides, Totem Animals, or with beings from the Fairy Realms, to promote feelings of safety and security (especially after physical or emotional abuse), to aid in recovery from addictions, to connect you with your inner child, to facilitate spiritual ascension, to aid in meditation, to promote psychic phenomena, and to open you to accepting the universal healing white light. This stone may include Amethyst, Citrine, or Clear Quartz.

QUARTZ, STRAWBERRY: Use at the 4th Chakra (Heart Chakra) to aid you in seeing the good in all beings, to encourage you to take time for the sweet things in life and to appreciate them, to enhance generosity by yourself or from others, and to connect you to your inner child.

QUARTZ, SUNSHINE AURA: Use at the 2nd Chakra (Sacral Chakra) or at the 3rd Chakra (Solar Plexus Chakra) to instill a sense of happiness and joy, to relieve the symptoms of Seasonal Affective Disorder, to enhance your self-esteem and personal power by providing a stable emotional platform from which to act, to aid in the absorption of nutrients, and for spiritual grounding.

QUARTZ, TANGERINE: Use at the 2nd Chakra (Sacral Chakra) to aid in recovery after a traumatic experience, to relieve the symptoms of P.T.S.D. (Post traumatic Stress Disorder), to facilitate past life healing, for karmic release, for emotional balance, to enhance your creativity, to work through self-limiting beliefs, to remove negative energy from the aura, to aid in manifesting prosperity and abundance, to aid in receiving accurate outcomes in divination practices, and to aid in channeling.

QUARTZ, TANZAN AURA: (Also known as Tanzine Aura Quartz, Tanzanite Aura Quartz, Celestial Aura Quartz, or as Indigo Aura Quartz) – Use at the 5th Chakra (Throat Chakra) or at the 6th Chakra (3rd Eye/Brow Chakra) to connect with beings from the angelic realm, to facilitate astral travel, for dream healing work, to ease feelings of grief, to aid in connecting with those on the other side, and to enhance intuitive guidance and the gift of foresight.

QUARTZ, TIBETAN: Use at the 1st Chakra (Root Chakra), 6th Chakra (3rd Eye/Brow Chakra), or at the 7th Chakra (Crown Chakra) to enhance your connection to your ancestors, to increase esoteric knowledge and an understanding of the occult, to facilitate astral travel, for protection while traveling, to facilitate an understanding of Tibetan Buddhist spiritual beliefs and ritualistic practices, to aid in karmic release, to facilitate a divine connection, to connect you to the element of water for emotional healing, to dissolve the ego consciousness and gain understanding of sunyata/shunyata, and to aid deeper states of meditation and of conscious awareness.

QUARTZ, TOURMALINATED: (Also known as Tourmaline-Included Quartz and Tourmalated Quartz) Use at the 1st Chakra (Root Chakra) or at the 7th Chakra (Crown Chakra) for grounding, to protect you against negative energies (amplified protection), to release stress and promote peace and calming, to balance mind, body, and spirit, to aid in self-acceptance, for physical healing, to cleanse body, mind, and spirit, and to balance the energies of the subtle body. This stone will also take on the properties of the type of Tourmaline that it includes (i.e. Black, Green, Pink, etc.).

QUARTZ, WITCH'S FINGER: Use at the 3rd Chakra (Solar Plexus Chakra) or at the 6th Chakra (3rd Eye/Brow Chakra) for enhancing the power of crystal layouts or grids, for protection, to balance the body, mind, and spirit, to enhance meditation, to aid in the channeling process, and to relieve the symptoms that accompany terminal illnesses.

-R-

RHODOCHROSITE: (Also known as Inca Rose) Use at the 4th Chakra (Heart Chakra) to stimulate the memory, to encourage empathy and a compassionate attitude, to instill confidence, and for emotional balance. Rhodochrosite is a good companion stone to Rhodonite. When used together, the two stones will enhance each other's energetic qualities.

RHODONITE: Use at the 4th Chakra (Heart Chakra) for encouraging love, to promote group cooperation, to reveal all aspects of a given situation, for grounding, to balance the mind, body, and spirit, to encourage successful meditation using mantras, to encourage new friendships, to stimulate generosity and the spirit of giving as well as gratitude, to heal the physical body as well as the emotions, to facilitate independence, to encourage compassion, empathy, and forgiveness, to aid in healing form past life experiences, to bring peace and calming, to enhance confidence, to heal wounds and insect bites, to reduce arthritis pain, & to ease the symptoms of shock. Rhodonite is a good companion stone to Rhodochrosite. When used together, the two stones will enhance each other's energetic qualities.

ROSELITE: Use at the 2nd Chakra (Sacral Chakra) or at the 4th Chakra (Heart Chakra) for enhancing romance, to increase passion, to encourage love to grow, to facilitate emotional bonding with another, and to balance the physical, emotional, and spiritual aspects of the self.

RUBY: (Also known as Red Corundum) Use at the 1st Chakra (Root Chakra) or at the 4th Chakra (Heart Chakra) to increase vitality, to enhance motivation, to stimulate Tantric energy, and to encourage the exploration of new thoughts and ideas.

RUBY-FUCHSITE: (Also known as Red Corundum-Included Fuchsite) Use at the 4th Chakra (Heart Chakra) for healing the mind, body, and spirit, for energetic balance, to manifest abundance, and to encourage compassion. This crystal contains Ruby and Fuchsite so it also displays the properties of these stones.

RUBY-KYANITE: (Also known as Red Corundum-Included Blue Kyanite) Use at the 1st Chakra (Root Chakra), 2nd Chakra (Sacral Chakra), or at the 4th Chakra (Heart Chakra) to cool anger and to balance the upper chakras with the lower chakras.

RUBY, STAR: (Also known as Red Star Corundum) Use at the 1st Chakra (Root Chakra), 4th Chakra (Heart Chakra), or at the 6th Chakra (3rd Eye/Brow Chakra) to enhance your vitality, to provide intuitive insights into your relationship with your partner, to promote a feeling of love and compassion for all beings, for protection, and to stimulate Tantric energy.

RUBY-ZOISITE: (Also known as Anyolite or as Red Corundum-Included Green Zoisite) Use at the 4th Chakra (Heart Chakra) for increasing vitality, to stimulate passion, for increasing motivation, to protect you against negative energies, to stimulate positive dreaming, to encourage accurate visions created by the pineal gland, to help transform negative energy into positive energy, to encourage your leadership qualities, to instill joy, to promote love, to instill courage, to increase physical and emotional strength, for detoxifying the body, to reduce fever, to maintain proper circulation, to stimulate altered states of consciousness, to balance body, mind, and spirit, for healing, to promote personal growth, to access the soul's past, to aid in past life ascension and regression, to encourage your unique characteristics, to promote oneness, and to enhance your auric field. This crystal contains Ruby and Green Zoisite so it also displays the properties of these stones.

RUTILE, GOLDEN: (Also known as Golden Angel Hair or as Golden Venus Hair) Use at the 7th Chakra (Crown Chakra) to help you to discover your divine nature, to bring the golden rays of the sun into the auric body, to disintegrate negative energy, and to enhance the power of prayer or meditation.

RUTILE, RED: (Also known as Red Angel Hair or as Red Venus Hair) Use at the 1st Chakra (Root Chakra), 2nd Chakra (Sacral Chakra), or at the 3rd Chakra (Solar Plexus Chakra) to increase fertility, to connect you with the energies of the earth, for grounding, to help cool the flames of anger, and to instill a sense of childlike wonder and curiosity.

RUTILE, SILVER: (Also known as Silver Angel Hair or as Silver Venus Hair) Use at the 6th Chakra (3rd Eye/Brow Chakra) to enhance your psychic energy and powers of intuition, to bring the celestial energies of the stars and the moon into the body, for dream healing practices, to promote safe astral travel, and for helping to make your wishes come true (as if they were wished upon a shooting star).

-S-

SALT, HIMALAYAN: Use at any chakra for general cleansing and purification or to promote peace and calming.

SAPPHIRE, BLUE: (Also known as Blue Corundum) Use at the 5th Chakra (Throat Chakra) or 6th Chakra (3rd Eye/Brow Chakra) to enhance communication with your spirit guides (especially Archangel Michael), to connect with your higher self, to facilitate psychic awareness and abilities, to promote a connection with the stars and to enhance your understanding of astrology, to increase your acceptance of universal happenings, and to reduce the undesired physical sensations that may accompany your spiritual awakening.

SAPPHIRE, BLUE STAR: (Also known as Blue Star Corundum) Use at the 6th Chakra (3rd Eye/Brow Chakra) or at the 7th Chakra (Crown Chakra) to open you to your intuitive powers and psychic awareness, to open you to divine healing energies, for spiritual ascension, to clear your energy field of attachments or imbalances, and to connect o with the wisdom of the universe and the Akashic Records.

SAPPHIRE, YELLOW: (Also known as Yellow Corundum) Use at the 3rd Chakra (Solar Plexus Chakra) for facilitating communication with Spirit guides and Totem Animals (especially Archangel Jophiel), to enhance spiritual illumination, to aid in instilling you with feelings of oneness, to promote self-love, to aid in enhancing concentration and in memorization, to heal the inner child, for protection, and to allow you to speak your mind.

SCAPOLITE, VIOLET: Use at the 4th Chakra (Heart Chakra) or at the 7th Chakra (Crown Chakra) to heal the heart after emotional trauma, to re-connect with your inner child (or to strengthen an existing connection), to instill a sense of joy and wonder, to facilitate playfulness and spontaneity, and for cleansing and purification of the energy body via the Violet Flame of St. Germaine.

SCHEELITE: Use at the 1st Chakra (Root Chakra) for grounding, to promote feelings of safety and security, for inner strength, to enhance courage, and to shield yourself from the negative thoughts and attitudes of others.

SCHIST: Use at the 2nd Chakra (Sacral Chakra), the 4th Chakra (Heart Chakra), or at the 6th Chakra (3rd Eye/Brow Chakra) to encourage a sense of child-like wonder, to aid you in appreciating the beauty in all things, to soften harsh personalities, to encourage you to connect with your emotional side, and to help you to shed old patterns and behaviors to change and grow for the good of all beings.

SCOLECITE: Use at the 7th Chakra (Crown Chakra) to open you to divine energy, to aid in channeling (to help to make the channel clear and open and to aid others present in correctly interpreting the messages that are given), for cleansing and purification of purification of body, mind, and spirit, to facilitate astral travel, to encourage spiritual growth and ascension, and to aid you in accessing and learning from the Akashic Records.

SELENITE, COLORLESS: (Also known as Colorless Gypsum) Use at the 7th Chakra (Crown Chakra) for purification, to cleanse the chakras and the aura, to promote a connection with your divine self, to aid in the ascension process, to clear the mind before meditation, to enhance your ability to follow your spiritual virtues, to bring the light into your being, and to promote peace and harmony.

SELENITE, GOLDEN: (Also known as Golden Gypsym) Use at the 7th Chakra (Crown Chakra) to bring the divine healing light of the universe into the body for powerful healing experiences, to cleanse and purify the body, mind, and spirit, to instill a sense of ultimate compassion in the user, to promote spiritual ascension and karmic evolution, to enhance meditation, and to facilitate astral travel.

SELENITE, ORANGE: (Also known as Orange Gypsum) Use at the 2nd Chakra (Sacral Chakra) or at the 4th Chakra (Heart Chakra) to balance the emotions, for protection (especially for highly sensitive people), for purification, to remove negative thinking, and to heal emotional wounds left from past lives.

SEPTARIAN NODULE: Use at the 1st Chakra (Root Chakra) or at the 2nd Chakra (Sacral Chakra) to promote bravery and courage, to calm fiery attitudes (anger, frustration, etc.), for grounding, to connect you with the energies of the fire element, to aid you in learning the importance self-control, to stabilize the emotional body, to aid in transformation (physical, emotional, and spiritual), and to help someone to become well-rounded. This stone is made of Golden Calcite and Brown Aragonite.

SERAPHINITE, BROWN: Use at the 1st Chakra (Root Chakra), 2nd Chakra (Sacral Chakra) or 4th Chakra (Heart Chakra) for removing thought patterns at a cellular and DNA level, to lift you up on Angel's wings during difficult times, for protection by your guardian angels and spirits, to promote inner strength, to enhance psychic insight, to bring order to chaotic situations and times in your life, to connect you with nature an d the elements, and to bring harmony and balance to your life. Brown Seraphinite is a recent find from Russia and is quite rare. If you are lucky enough to have this stone enter your life, it should be kept close and held dear.

SERAPHINITE, GREEN: Use at the 4th Chakra (Heart Chakra) to heal body, mind, and spirit, to promote a connection with the angelic realm, and to instill a feeling of completion.

SERPENTINE: (Also known as New Jade) Use at the 4th Chakra (Heart Chakra) for aiding in meditation, to enhance psychic powers, to clear a pathway for the kundalini, to aid in past life regression and ascension, to create balance between the mind, body, and spirit, to aid in intending to direct energy to heal the physical body, to cleanse the physical body, to aid in the assimilation of nutrients, to aid in connection with the angelic realm, to promote compassion, and to relieve muscle pain.

SHATTUCKITE: Use at the 6th Chakra (3rd Eye/Brow Chakra) to enhance intuition, for connecting the user with the energy of the cosmos, to access the Akashic Records, and for protection during astral travel and shamanic journeying.

SHELL, ABALONE: (Also known as Abalone, as Rainbow Mother of Pearl, as Paua Shell, or as Ear Shell) Use at any chakra to balance and harmonize the energies of the body, to repair the aura, and to instill a sense of childlike wonder in adults.

SHELL, SHIVA'S EYE: (Also known as Shell, Turban Snail or as Shell, Pacific Cat's Eye) to facilitate creativity, to promote self-expression (verbally or through the arts), to connect you with Lord Shiva, to enhance your masculine energy, and to enhance the positive energy in your environment and surroundings.

SHIVA LINGAM STONES: (Also known as Lingham Stones, as Lingam Stones, as Shiva Linghams, as Shiva Lingams, as Shiva Lingham Stones, as Lingams, or as Linghams) Use at the 1st Chakra (Root Chakra) or at the 2nd Chakra (Sacral Chakra) to increase fertility, to bring balance between the male and female energies of the body, to enhance your feeling of personal power and control over your life situations, for worship and praise of Lord Shiva, to increase personal strength and will-power, and to stimulate sexual or creative energies.

SHUNGITE: Use at the 3rd Chakra (Solar Plexus Chakra), 6th Chakra (3rd Eye/Brow Chakra), or at the 7th Chakra (Crown Chakra) to facilitate Astral Travel; to aid you in feeling a connection with all beings; to promote feelings of universal oneness; to create a protective shield around the energy body to defend you against EMFs or psychic attack; to help bring a light to dark times in your life; to help regulate the temperature of the body; to energize body, mind, and spirit; to transmute negative energy into positive energy; and to reduce pain and inflammation.

SILVER: Use at the 2nd Chakra (Sacral Chakra) or at the 6th Chakra (3rd Eye/Brow Chakra) for enhancing intuition, to connect you with the water element, to aid in enhancing female energy, for emotional balance, allows you to look at situations objectively, to aid you in the ability to return to the physical body after astral travel, to connect you with lunar energies, and to open and clear your energetic meridians.

SODALITE: Use at the 5th Chakra (Throat Chakra) or at the 6th Chakra (3rd Eye/Brow Chakra) for increasing accurate intuitive thoughts, to encourage successful stilling of the mind during meditation, to bring out the truth in any situation, to help you to stand up for you, for protection from electromagnetic pollution, to enhance group cooperation, to aid in speaking your truth, to banish habits and negative thinking patterns, to aid in absorbing new information, to remove fear, to banish guilt, to encourage confidence, to encourage a healthy metabolism, to remove insomnia, and to reduce fevers.

SPINEL, PINK: Use at the 1st Chakra (Root Chakra) or at the 4th Chakra (Heart Chakra) to enhance vitality, to enhance passion for your partner, to aid the body in using antioxidants to prevent cancer, to repair damaged cells in the body, and to help you to feel the oneness among all beings in the universe.

STAUROLITE: (Also known as Fairy Cross or as Fairy Tear) Use at the 4th Chakra (Heart Chakra) for balance (physical, emotional, and spiritual), to align the chakras, to encourage healthy grieving, to establish a connection with the divine, to promote emotional healing and stability, to heal childhood trauma, and to facilitate a connection with earth spirits (fairies, sprites, nymphs, etc.).

STIBNITE: (Also known as Stibinite) Use at the 1st Chakra (Root Chakra) for protection, to relieve physical pain (especially in the joints), to draw up energy from the earth when you are feeling energetically depleted, to allow you to recognize your fears and to provide insight in how to overcome them, and to shield and protect the aura.

STICHITITE: (Also known as Stichtite) Use this stone at the 6th Chakra (3rd Eye/Brow Chakra) or at the 7th Chakra (Crown Chakra) to connect with the Divine cosmic energy, to enhance meditation, to tap into the knowledge of ancient cultures and peoples, and to aid in holding the intention to act for the highest good of all.

STILBITE, PEACH: Use at the 2nd Chakra (Sacral Chakra) or at the 4th Chakra (Heart Chakra) to help heal problems of the heart (physical or emotional), to aid you in working through the grieving process, to aid in removing symptoms of many common skin problems (i.e. acne, eczema, rosacea, etc.), and to instill a sense of self-worth and self-love.

SUGILITE: (Also known as Sugelite, Sugalite, Lavulite, Luvulite, and Royal Azel) Use at the 7th Chakra (Crown Chakra to aid in opening you to divine energy, to enhance meditation, to promote astral travel, to stimulate lucid dreaming and dream healing, to aid you in learning and understanding shamanic practices and rituals, to communicate with your ancestors or spirit guides, and to aid in working with the Violet Flame of St. Germaine.

SUNSTONE: Use at the 2nd Chakra (Sacral Chakra) or 3rd Chakra (Solar Plexus Chakra) to instill joy and happiness, to manifest abundance, to promote a positive self-image and self confidence, to encourage inner strength, to enhance feelings of gratitude and your willingness to share, to bring light to dark or negative thoughts, for psychological healing, to stimulate creativity, to aid in digestion and problems associated with the sexual organs, to counter the effects of Seasonal Affective Disorder (S.A.D.), to warm the heart and soul, to balance the mind, body, and spirit, and to promote a positive attitude.

SUPER SEVEN (TM): (Also known as Melody's Stone or as Super 7) Use at the 6th Chakra (3rd Eye/Brow Chakra) or 7th Chakra (Crown Chakra) for facilitating spiritual ascension, to promote Lovingkindness, to enhance your intuitive abilities, to aid in astral travel, for cleansing cords, to remove negativity, to aid in increasing your psychic awareness, to promote the opening of the chakras, and to aid in channeling the universal knowledge of the healing properties of crystals and minerals.

-T-

TANZANITE: (Also known as Blue Zoisite) Use at the 5th Chakra (Throat Chakra) or 6th Chakra (3rd Eye/Brow Chakra) to stimulate intuition, to enhance the powers of telepathy, to facilitate communication with your spirit guides, totem animals, or guardian angels, to create a connection to the universe and to the divine, to enhance psychic awareness, to bring peace, calming, and serenity, to promote deep states of meditation, to facilitate astral travel and out-of-body experiences, and to quicken the ascension process.

THOMSONITE: Use at the 2nd Chakra (Sacral Chakra) or at the 4th Chakra (Heart Chakra) to cleanse and purify the physical body, to heal disorders relating to the internal organs, to relieve gastric upset, to clear the body of intestinal parasites, to instill a compassionate attitude toward animals, and to reduce the size and spread of cancerous growths.

THULITE: (Also known as Pink Zoisite) Use at the 2nd Chakra (Sacral Chakra) or at the 4th Chakra (Heart Chakra) to heal emotional wounds, to promote self-love, for forgiveness, for enhancing inner-child work, and for healing and repairing relationships of all kinds.

TIGER IRON: Use at the 1st Chakra (Root Chakra) or 2nd Chakra (Sacral Chakra) for grounding, for protection, to instill creative energy in artists (especially for painters), for grounding, to bring your astral body back to earth after astral travel or dream work, to provide strength during difficult times, to boost your vitality and increase your life force energy, to enhance self-confidence and will power, to enhance inner-strength, to aid in focus and concentration, for healing the physical body, and to balance the influence of the elements on your body. This stone is a composition of Golden Tiger's Eye, Red Jasper, and Hematite.

TIGER'S EYE, BLUE: (Also known as Hawk's Eye or as Crocidolite) Use at the 3rd Chakra (Solar Plexus Chakra), the 5th Chakra (Throat Chakra), or at the 6th Chakra (3rd Eye/Brow Chakra) for grounding, to increase psychic powers, to encourage the rising of the kundalini through the chakras, for protection, to instill inner-strength, to stimulate compassion, to aid you in sorting through details and to aid in completing tedious tasks, to aid in removing negative habits, to banish depression, to heal the eyes, to treat disorders of the reproductive system, for balancing the chakras, to aid in healing broken bones, to aid in communication, for peace and calming, and to banish fears of all kinds.

TIGER'S EYE, GOLDEN: Use at the 3rd Chakra (Solar Plexus Chakra) for grounding, to increase psychic powers, to encourage the rising of the kundalini through the chakras, for protection, to stimulate compassion, to aid you in sorting through details and to aid in completing tedious tasks, to pull together many details in order to make sense of a whole, to aid in removing negative habits, to instill self-confidence and inner-strength, to promote equality, to banish depression, to heal the eyes, to treat disorders of the reproductive system, to aid in healing broken bones, to help you succeed on tests and exams, & to encourage success in business meetings.

TIGER'S EYE, RED: (Also known as Falcon's Eye, Dragon's Eye, or as Ox Eye) Use at the 1st Chakra (Root Chakra) or at the 3rd Chakra (Solar Plexus Chakra) for grounding, to increase psychic powers, to encourage the rising of the kundalini through the chakras, for protection, to stimulate compassion, to aid you in sorting through details and to aid in completing tedious tasks, to aid in removing negative habits, to banish depression, to heal the eyes, to encourage sensible actions, to treat disorders of the reproductive system, to aid in healing broken bones, to increase vitality, and to encourage motivation.

TOPAZ, BLUE: Use at the 5th Chakra (Throat Chakra) to facilitate communication with your Guardian Angel, to connect one with the water element, to stimulate your intuition and psychic powers, to help you go with the flow and be open to what the universe has to offer, to help you to channel your creative energies in a positive manner, and to heal problems associated with the throat and adrenals.

TOPAZ, LEMON: Use at the 3rd Chakra (Solar Plexus Chakra) to instill happiness and joy, to relieve the symptoms of Seasonal Affective Disorder (S.A.D.) by bringing the light of the sun into the physical body, to promote inner strength and courage, and to promote the absorption of vitamins and antioxidants.

TOPAZ, IMPERIAL GOLDEN: (Also known as Topaz, Imperial Golden and as Topaz, Golden Imperial) Use at the 3rd Chakra (Solar Plexus Chakra) and at the 7th Chakra (Crown Chakra) to bring the divine light of spirit into the body, to neutralize cancerous cells within the body, to open the crown chakra, to enhance meditation, to aid in forgiving you as well as others, and to relieve symptoms of upset stomach, digestive pain or discomfort, or gastric upset.

TOURMALINE, BLACK: (Also known as Schorl or as Aphrizite) Use at the 1st Chakra (Root Chakra) for protection against electromagnetic pollution and negative energy, grounding, increased physical energy, to banish negative thoughts, to enhance positive thinking and creativity, to protect you from electromagnetic frequencies, to strengthen the immune system, for cleansing the physical and ethereal bodies, and to aid in decreasing arthritis pain.

TOURMALINE, BLUE: (Also known as Indicolite or as Indigolite) Use at the 6th Chakra (3rd Eye/ Brow Chakra) to stimulate the intuition, to bring clarity to your intuitive insights, to aid you in staying in the present moment by promoting conscious awareness, to aid in the decision-making process, to facilitate communication (especially when communicating your psychic insights or "predictions" to another person), to aid you in being compassionate to all beings (by way of the 3rd eye you are able to put yourself in another's shoes in order to better understand that person's actions or behaviors), and to keep the 3rd eye focused on one thing at a time so as to keep you from feeling scattered or overwhelmed with information.

TOURMALINE, BROWN (DRAVITE): (Also known as Champagne Tourmaline or as Brown Dravide Tourmaline) Use at the 1st Chakra (Base Chakra/Root Chakra) or at the 2nd Chakra (Sacral Chakra) for protection, to ground the energy/spirit body in the physical world, to detox the physical body, to relieve pain from sore feet, to encourage better eating habits, and to remind you to celebrate life (even in it more challenging moments). This is also a great stone to use at the Earth Star Chakra for grounding and absorption of Earth energies. This stone reminds yo to be present in the moment and find the gifts in today.

TOURMALINE, GREEN (ELBAITE): (Also known as Verdite, Verdelite, Verdalite, Verdalite Tourmaline, Verdite Tourmaline, or as Verdelite Tourmaline) Use at the 4th Chakra (Heart Chakra) for balancing the chakras, for protection from negative energy, for healing the mind, body, and spirit, to instill virtuous behavior, for personal growth, for spiritual ascension, and to connect you with nature.

TOURMALINE, GREEN (UVITE): Use at the 1st Chakra (Root Chakra) or at the 4th Chakra (Heart Chakra) to attract wealth, prosperity, and abundance, to help you to attract wealth, prosperity, and abundance, to help you in determining your appropriate career path, to banish envy, to deter greed, to instill a sense of gratitude in the user, to enhance the feng shui in a room by moving chi (life force energy), and to promote balance and harmony.

TOURMALINE, PINK (ELBAITE): Use at the 4th Chakra (Heart Chakra) for encouraging love, for emotional healing, for balancing the mind, body, and spirit, for enhancing friendships, and for promoting feelings of safety and security. The properties are for light to medium Pink Elbaite Tourmaline crystals. For information on the deep pink crystal properties, please see "Tourmaline, Red (Elbaite)" below.

TOURMALINE, RED (ELBAITE): (Also known as Rubellite Tourmaline) Use at the 1st Chakra (Root Chakra) or at the 4th Chakra (Heart Chakra), to enhance motivation, for encouraging you to pursue your passions, to remove "spiritual roadblocks", to awaken the heart chakra, to enhance feelings of compassion and oneness, and to connect to the energy of the Goddess Quan Yin (goddess of lovingkindness).

TOURMALINE, VIOLET: (Also known as Mozambique Tourmaline or as Cuprian Tourmaline) Use at the 4th Chakra (Heart Chakra) for aiding in the spiritual ascension process, to release karmic debts, to cool the heat of anger, and for balancing the body, mind, and spirit.

TOURMALINE, WATERMELON: Use at the 4th Chakra (Heart Chakra) for balancing the mind, body, and spirit, for balancing the chakras, to promote peace, calming, and tranquility, to instill joyfulness, to enhance gratitude, and to comfort you during difficult times. This stone is a combination of Green Tourmaline and Pink Tourmaline found in the same stone.

TURQUOISE: Use at the 4th Chakra (Heart Chakra) or at the 5th Chakra (Throat Chakra) for enhancing communication with beings from other realms, to enhance self expression and communication, to help you to be mindful of the present moment, to help you to live in the moment, to remove negativity from you and your environment, to enhance self confidence, to relieve symptoms of acid reflux or heartburn, to aid in relaxation, for spiritual ascension, to help you to remain on the path for his/her highest good, to boost the immune system, to aid in healing ailments of the eyes, to reduce acidity in the body and aid in detoxification, and to reduce inflammation.

TURQUOISE, SLEEPING BEAUTY: Use at the 4th Chakra (Heart Chakra), 5th Chakra (Throat Chakra), or at the 6th Chakra (3rd Eye/Brow Chakra), to protect the energy body of the user, to facilitate communication between the user and your ancestors, to promote astral travel, to encourage journeying and healing while in the dream state, to enhance your clairvoyant abilities (psychic sight), to help treat sleep disorders (especially insomnia), and to promote feelings of peace and tranquility.

-U-

ULEXITE: (Also known as T.V. Stone, T.V. Rock, Television Stone, or as Television Rock) Use at the 7th Chakra (Crown Chakra) to bring clarity and lucidity to all activities (especially those requiring intense concentration), to raise your energetic vibration, to help you to see the hidden meaning in a situation, and to aid you during the ascension process.

UNAKITE: (Also known as Epidote with Feldspar) Use at the 4th Chakra (Heart Chakra) for creating emotional balance, to stimulate compassion and empathy, to encourage gratitude, for spiritual ascension, to establish a connection with nature (especially with the plant kingdom), to balance chakra energy, to instill determination, to balance the male and female energies within the body, to eliminate co-dependence in relationships (and for gaining new-found independence once you clearly see both the masculine and feminine aspects within yourself), to aid in working through the emotions surrounding a "break-up" or divorce, and to facilitate feelings of love and friendship.

-V-

VANADINITE: Use at the 1st Chakra (Root Chakra) or 2nd Chakra (Sacral Chakra) to increase vitality, to strengthen the immune system, to aid in detoxifying the physical body, to aid in assimilation of vitamins and nutrients, to manifest prosperity and abundance, to create lasting bonds between family and friends, to enhance creativity in artistic endeavors, and to instill joy.

VARISCITE: Use at the 1st Chakra (Root Chakra) and at the 4th Chakra (Heart Chakra) to promote playfulness, to connect with Earth spirits, for instilling a sense of child-like wonder, to promote inner peace, to encourage the act of meditation, and for earth healing.

VESUVIANITE, PURPLE: (Also known as Purple Idocrase) Use at the 1st Chakra (Root Chakra), 4th Chakra (Heart Chakra), or at the 7th Chakra (Crown Chakra) to instill love and compassion for all beings, to help you recognize the oneness of all things, to connect you with the Goddess Quan Yin, and to transform fiery or aggressive energy into positive energy.

-W-

WULFENITE: Use at the 2nd Chakra (Sacral Chakra) or at the 3rd Chakra (Solar Plexus Chakra) to facilitate a connection with your totem animal(s), to increase strength and vitality, to balance the emotions, to aid in grounding, to banish negative thoughts from your mind, and to balance the fire element in some astrological signs.

-Y-

YOUNGITE: Use at the 4th Chakra (Heart Chakra) to instill a sense of childlike wonder, for physical rejuvenation, to reduce the signs of aging, and to bring magic into mundane tasks.

-Z-

ZEBRA STONE: (Also known as Zebra Marble, Zebra Jasper, and as Zebra Rock) Use at the 1st Chakra (Root Chakra) or at the 7th Chakra (Crown Chakra) to balance yin and yang energies in the body, to balance the male and female aspects of the self, for promoting harmony and tranquility, to instill ancient wisdom and values, to promote love for your shadow side and help it to grow toward the light, to facilitate a connection with your totem animal or spirit animal guide, and to balance the body, mind, and spirit.

ZINCITE, GREEN: Use at the 4th Chakra (Heart Chakra) for enhancing inner strength, to enhance energetic healing, to stimulate intuition, and to promote harmony and cooperation within groups.

ZIRCON, BROWN: Use at the 1st Chakra (Root Chakra) to balance the elemental energies in your body or environment, to call in the wisdom and energy of the four directions, to enhance ceremony and ritual, for earth healing, for grounding, for emotional stability, and to help you connect with nature.

ZOISITE, GREEN: Use at the 4th Chakra (Heart Chakra) to refresh the body and mind, to heal the heart chakra, to enhance masculine energy, for balance, to help treat symptoms associated with digestive upset (nausea, heartburn, excess gas, Irritable Bowel Syndrome, etc.), to connect you with your totem animals (especially for receiving Bee medicine), and for general health and wellbeing.

ABUNDANCE QUARTZ: (Also known as Prosperity Quartz or as Manifestation Quartz) This formation helps you to draw in abundance in all forms. Whether you are looking to manifest prosperity, love, compassion, healing, creativity, etc. this Quartz formation will add a powerful boost of positive energy to your intentions, dreams, and wishes! It works especially well when places in the center of a crystal grid.

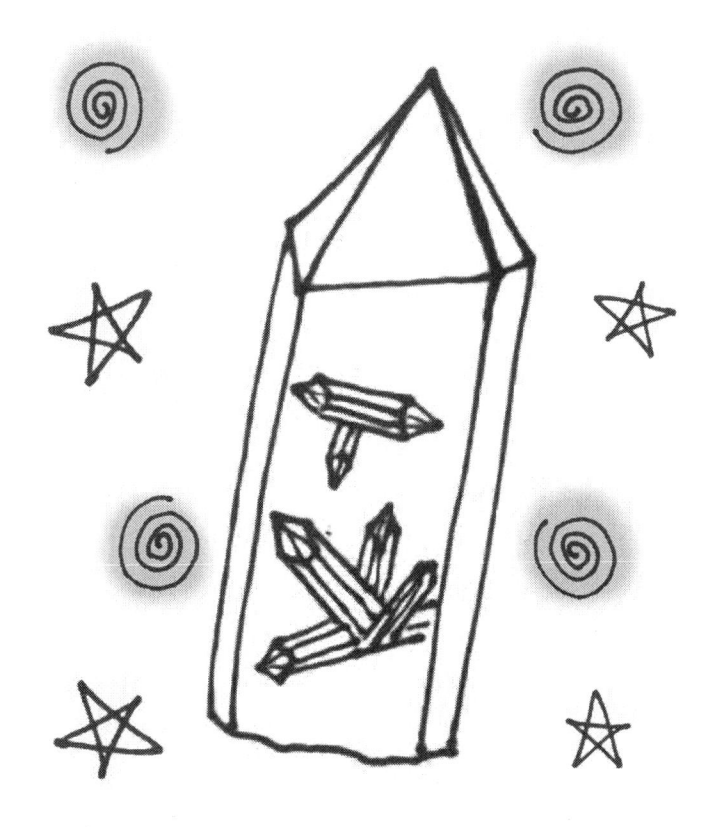

BARNACLE QUARTZ: (Also known as Fairy Dust Quartz)

This formation is identified by many small crystals growing along one or more of the main crystal's sides (looking like a glittery dust on the styour surface and mimicking barnacles growing on a ship's hull). They are great for de-cluttering (physically and mentally). They are also perfect for detoxing the physical body and for cellular and DNA-level repair. Additionally, they can help you see through to the truth in a situation (sometimes realizing that not all that glitters is gold).

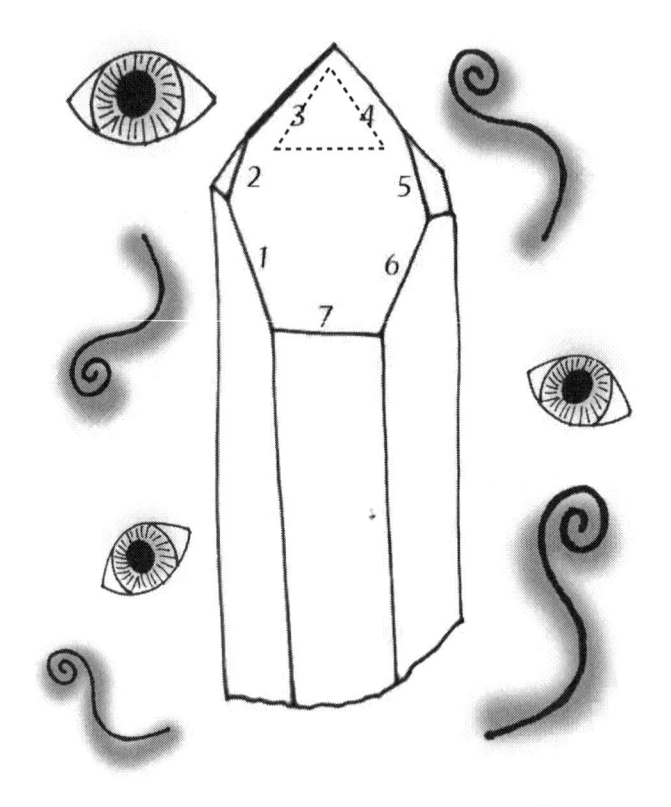

CHANNELING QUARTZ: (Also known as Channeler Quartz) This Quartz formation can be identified in a way similar to identifying a Dow crystal. The main face of the crystal will have seven edges and there will be a small face with three edges directly opposite (behind) the main face. These special crystals have truly amazing energy. They are especially useful for intuitives, mediums, or anyone needing some psychic insight. They are best used placed to the Third Eye in meditation, allowing messages, symbols, or images to flow into the mind.

CLUSTER QUARTZ: This is a group of crystal points that have grown sharing a common matrix or host rock. Clusters are composed of many crystal points that are all attached to a base (typically composed on matrix rock or substrate). Often, crystal clusters are just a part of a large geode. Clusters can be used to send energy in all directions. They emit a strong healing vibration and are good for clearing room spaces as well as for clearing other stones. Clusters can be used for manifesting, or to promote cooperation, unity, and harmony. They can also be used to concentrate energy in one area. These are very diverse healing tools.

DOLPHIN QUARTZ:

These stones are simply adorable and are very easy to identify. They are comprised of a large crystal with a smaller crystal attached to one of the sides of the larger stone (like a small, baby dolphin attached to its mother). There may be one or more crystals attached (usually growing in the same direction as the main crystal, as opposed to barnacle crystals which grow in all directions). In this case, the baby crystal is along for the ride, which is similar to how these crystals work for healing. They can take us on great journeys (internal or external). They also help you to learn to "go with the flow". Additionally, they are great for facilitating emotional release.

ÐOW QUARTZ: This Quartz formation was named for Jane Ann Dow (channel and crystal healer). It can be identified by it's characteristic 7-3-7-3-7-3 formation. This means that each of the crystal's six facets (or faces) will have either seven or three edges (alternating). Using this crystal helps us to dissolve the boundary between our inner and outer worlds, helping us to realize that we are one with everything in our universe. These crystals also help us to recognize our own divine nature and can facilitate our spiritual growth and connection with Divine energy. They are also great for balancing the chakras and for removing energy blockages from the body. They can also be used in meditation with amazing results! All Dow Crystals are Channeling Crystals.

DRUZY QUARTZ

Also known as Druzy crystals, this term refers to very tiny crystals that often appear to be just a rough, sparkly surface where individual crystal points cannot be seen. Crystal druse is formed when the liquid mineral solution from which the crystals are created cools very rapidly so that the crystals do not have much time to form (as opposed to large crystals which are typically formed during a slow cooling process). Crystal druse may also be formed when silica-rich water evaporates from a mineral pocket, leaving tiny crystals on the surface of any existing stone. Druzy crystals represent "attitudes of gratitude" and help you learn not to take things for granted. They remind you that even the small things in your life can be very powerful.

ELESTIAL QUARTZ:

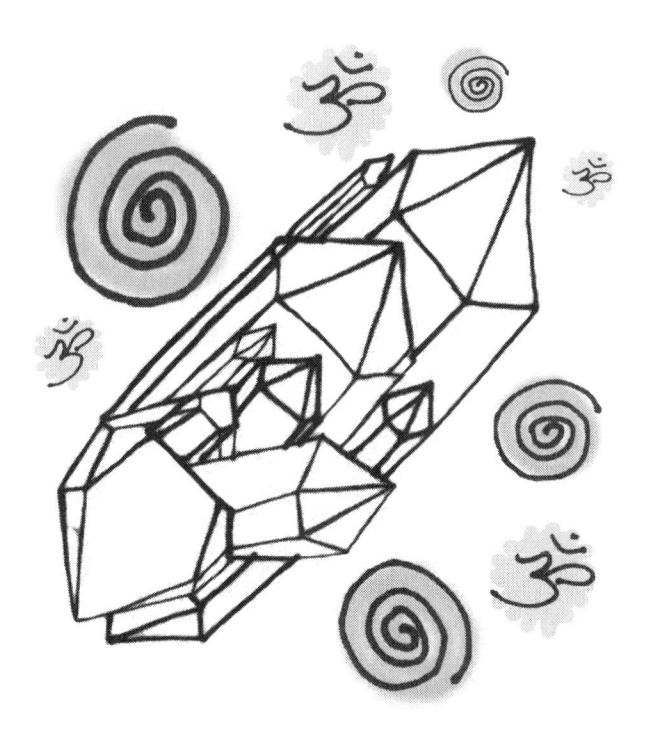

This is a crystal formation that is also known as a Heavenly Crystal, a Jacare Crystal, a Skeletal Crystal, an Alligator Crystal, or as a Crocodile Crystal. Elestial crystals can be identified by small crystals growing on the faces and sides of a larger crystal or crystal cluster, where all of the smaller crystals are growing parallel to the main crystal. These crystals have a very ethereal energy and are great for enhancing things like meditation, shamanic journeying, and astral travel. These crystals are sometimes thought of as the "bones of the earth".

ETCHED QUARTZ

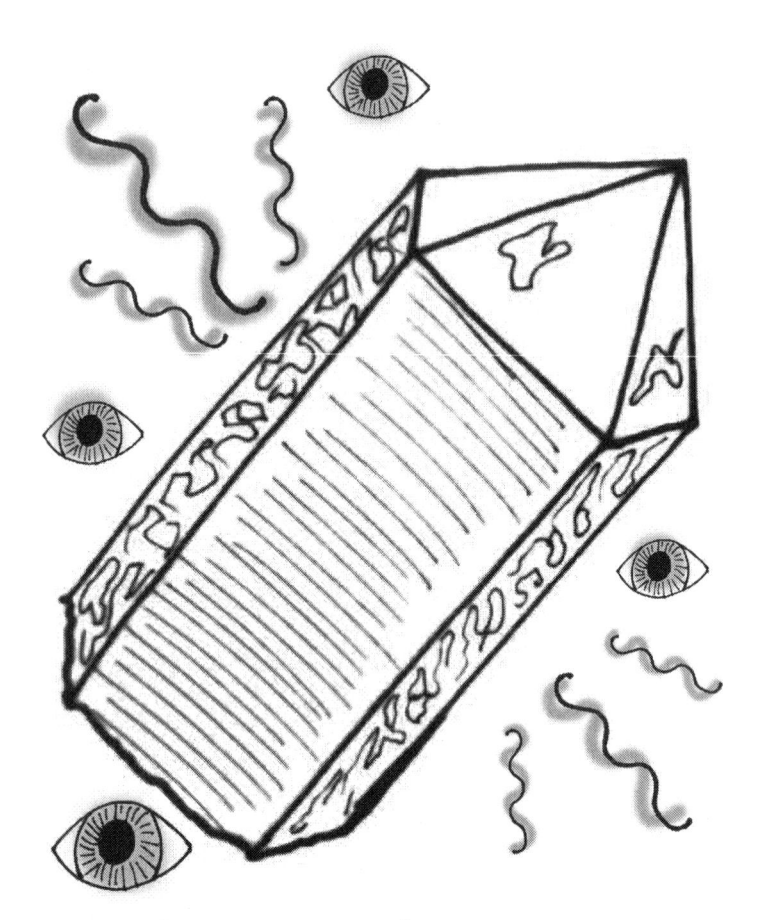

These crystals display strange patterns on their surfaces, appearing sometimes like images and other times like strange writing. Some say this is the writing of angels, others say this is information placed into the crystal by ancient civilizations. It is said that the information or images may be accessed through meditation when used by someone with positive intention who strives to work for the highest good of all. The messages received may be personal or planetary in nature.

GENERATOR QUARTZ: These crystals can be identified by six sides (of equal size) and six facets (of equal size) that join into a perfect point at the terminated end of the crystal. These crystals can be used to draw energy into a space, to ground energy, or to direct and focus channeled healing energy. They also act to enhance group cooperation and efforts toward a common goal. These crystals may be natural or cut and polished. Generators are used to harness and focus energy. These work especially well when used in the center of a crystal grid.

ISIS QUARTZ: (Also known as Goddess Quartz or as Teacher Quartz) These are those crystals in which one of the facets (or faces) has five edges with the top two edges usually elongated (forming a tall point). These crystals are a go-to stone for emotional healing of any kind (especially for issues relating back to lack of self-love or for aiding with the grieving process). They can be used to reclaim your power when it has been given away to another (consciously or not). They help you to connect to the energy of the Divine Feminine and bring balance to the masculine and feminine energies in the body, mind, and spirit. They embody the spirit of the Egyptian Goddess, Isis, bringing her wisdom and gentle, nurturing guidance to the earth plane, where it can be utilized and integrated into your life.

KEY QUARTZ:

(Also known as Portal Quartz or as Crater Quartz) These crystals can be identified by an indented marking (formed when another crystal grew into the stone and was then separated). These markings (often called keys) are usually six-sided (capturing the impression of the crystal point that made the mark) and may be large or small, deep or shallow, depending upon the amount of contact between the two crystals involved. These stones can be useful for manifesting (as the keys act like centers for accumulating energy). They can also be used as portals to other dimensions or realms and are especially useful when you are in need of communication with higher beings (i.e. Ascended Masters, Archangels, Totem Animals, Spirit Guides, etc.).

MANIFESTATION QUARTZ: (Also

known as Mother-with-Child Quartz, as Inner Child Quartz or as Inner Self Quartz). This formation can be identified by a small crystal growing completely inside of a larger crystal. This is relatively rare and so these crystals can be difficult to find. These crystals are best used for manifesting or for actualizing your desires, for healing the inner self, for inner child work, to facilitate communication with the inner self, to enhance inner knowing, for aiding in fertility and conception, as well as for successfully carrying a pregnancy to term without difficulty.

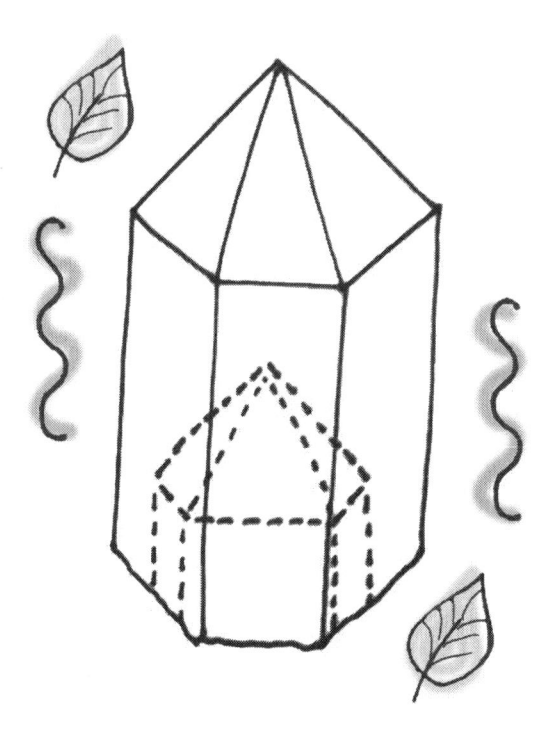

$\mathcal{P}HA\mathcal{N}TOM$ $QUARTZ$: Phantoms are

identified as faint crystal images found within crystals. They are created when a crystal stops growing, is covered with another mineral substance, and then resumes growth. The thin mineral layer becomes trapped and creates a "phantom" crystal image of a particular growth stage. These crystals can be used for inner growth, enhancing intuition, and spiritual ascension and evolution.

RAINBOW QUARTZ: These crystals are identified by inner rainbow prisms (often caused by fractures or inclusions/occlusions). These have been known to symbolize happiness and optimism. They also act as a bridge between worlds. When crystals contain a rainbow inside, it usually is a sign that the Deva (spirit) within the crystal is ready to make a connection with you.

RECORD-KEEPER QUARTZ: These

crystals can be identified by the appearance of raised or sunken record-keepers most-commonly found on the faces of a crystal. These crystals are often used to access the knowledge and wisdom of ancient civilizations and peoples (or of your ancestors). They are also used for accessing information in the Akashic Records and for enhancing any type of past life healing work.

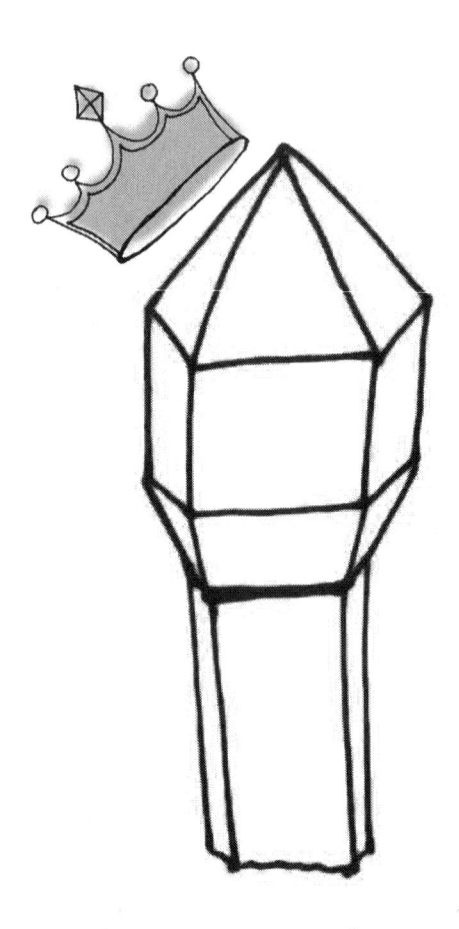

SCEPTER QUARTZ: Scepter formations

can be easily identified by a large crystal point that has formed around the tip of a central crystal shaft. This formation resembles the scepter held by royalty. These are powerful crystal tools which are often used for directing intense energy during psychic surgery or for ritual work or ceremony. Scepters may be either single- or double terminated.

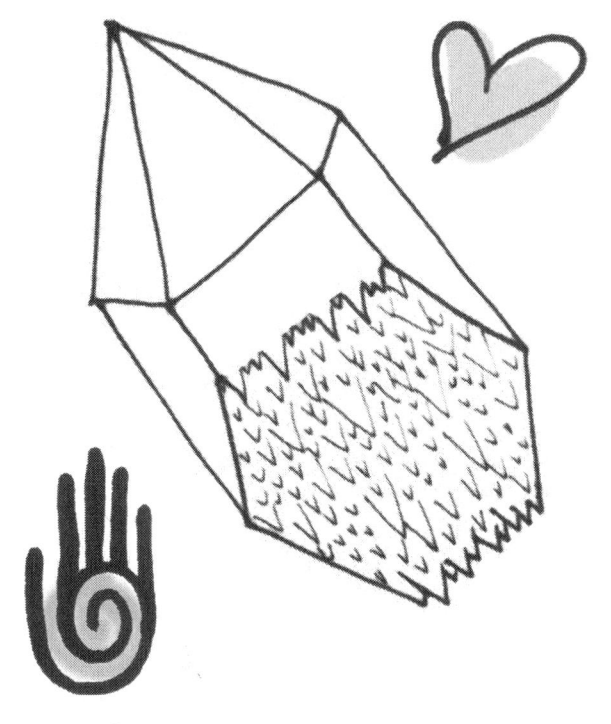

SELF-HEALED QUARTZ:

This formation can be identified by tiny, triangular crystal points growing along what used to be a broken surface of the crystal. These tiny points grow over the exposed portion of the break, "healing" the broken surface of the crystal. These crystals are used for any kind of self-healing work, especially for enhancing self-love. They are also great for those who are suffering feelings of "burn-out" at their jobs (especially for healers, care-givers, nurses, counselors, etc).

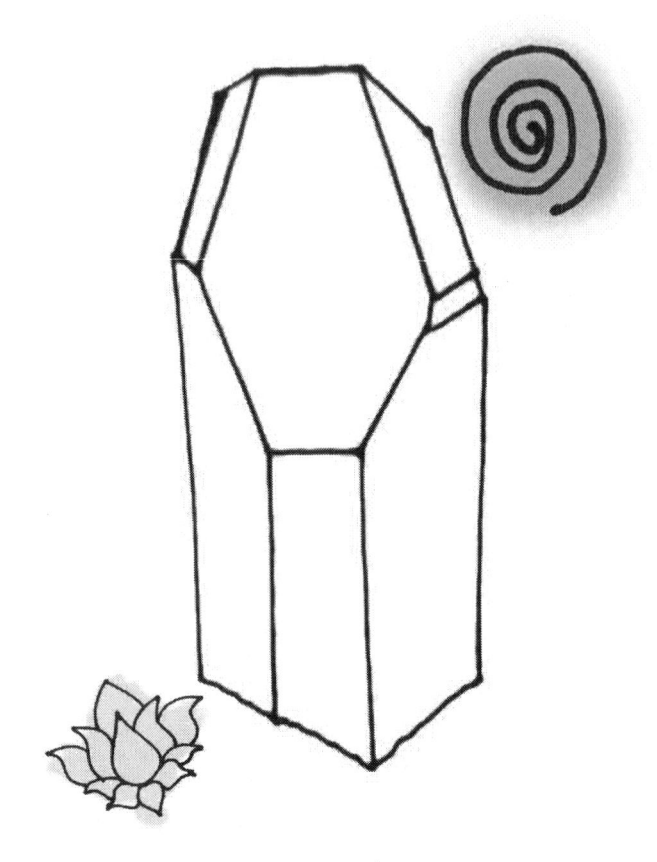

SHOVEL QUARTZ: (Also known as Spade

Quartz) This formation is identified as crystal that exhibits a wide, flat main face with a blunt tip. The blunt tip is not broken, but has naturally formed in a "spade" shape. Crystals of this formation are used to enhance meditation as well as for digging through layers of trauma or emotional wounds to uncover the gift in your experiences (which can help you to work through them).

SOUL-MATE QUARTZ: These crystals are very similar to the Twin Quartz formation, but they are connected so deeply that the connection goes beyond sharing just one side. This formation displays two crystals, interwoven and intertwined so that they are seen as one crystal with two points. These crystals are a metaphor for the true connection felt by soul mates. They can be used for strengthening, enhancing, or repairing a soul-mate relationship (whether the relationship is romantic or not). they can also help you to find your soul mate in this lifetime (as well as see past and future lifetime connections with your soul mate). Additionally, these crystals can also help you to integrate lessons that are learned from your soul mate relationship.

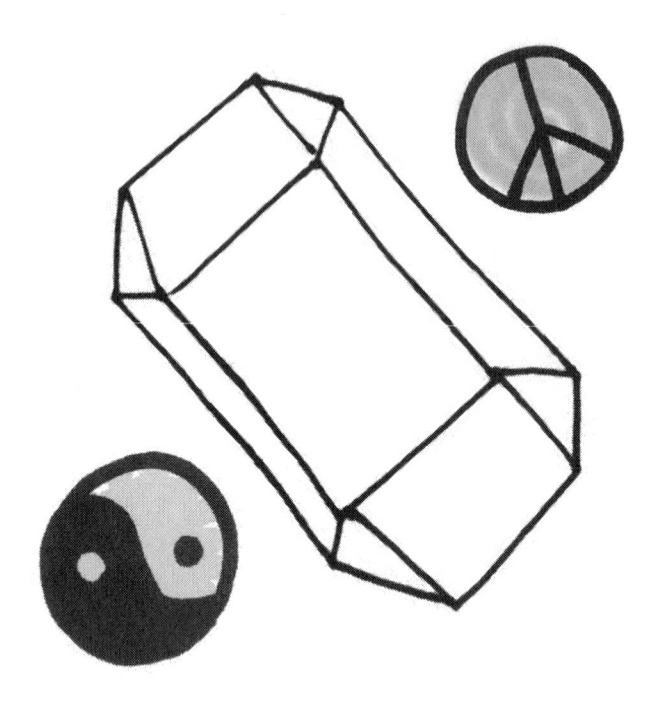

TABULAR QUARTZ: (Also known as Tabby

Quartz) These crystals are easily identified by their flat, wide shape. They can be used to promote communication. In addition, they are frequently used to promote equilibrium and balance (between two people, concepts, energy centers, body parts, etc.). These are almost always found as natural crystals, but they may be cut and polished. Faden Quartz is almost always found in a tabula formation (please see page 90 for more information about Faden Quartz).

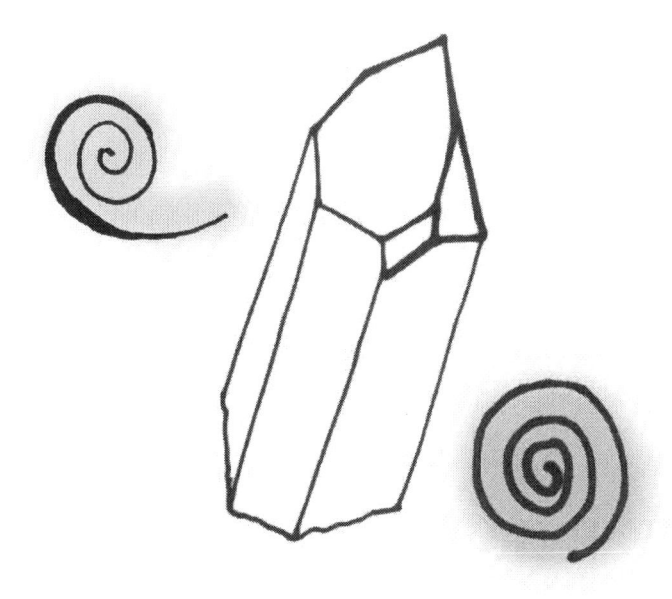

TIME LINE QUARTZ (FUTURE):

(Also known as Future Time Link Quartz, or as Activation Right Quartz) These crystals can be identified by an extra facet (rhombus-shaped) just below the crystal's six facets (or faces). The top of this seventh (extra), rhombus-shaped facet points to the right. The energy in this formation spirals clockwise from the base of the crystal toward its point. These crystals are extremely projective and send and amplify energy. They can be used to send energy to the body and so are effective tools for healing others. These crystals act as links to the future, bringing useful information (through intuitive insight) for decision-making. Additionally, they can help you to access the information in the Akashic Records.

TIME LINE QUARTZ (PAST): (Also

known as Past Time Link Quartz, or as Activation Left Quartz) These crystals can be identified by an extra facet (rhombus-shaped) just below the crystal's six facets (or faces). The top of this seventh (extra), rhombus-shaped facet points to the left. The energy in this formation spirals counter-clockwise from the base of the crystal toward its point. These crystals are extremely receptive and absorb and gather energy. They can be used to send energy to the body and so are effective tools for healing others. These crystals act as links to the past, bringing useful information for past life healing as well as for healing your ancestral line. Additionally, they can help you to access the information in the Akashic Records.

TWIN QUARTZ: These crystals are identified as a pair of crystals of similar size that have grown together (typically sharing a side). These crystals are representative of relationships and enhance feelings of being connected to "All That Is." This crystal formation occurs naturally. These crystals work very well for any kind of soul mate healing work. Additionally, they help reveal lessons from your light side and your shadow side (offering understanding and clarity about the two halves, but also of the whole).

WINDOW QUARTZ: These crystals can be identified by an extra diamond-shaped facet located just below the main crystal face. This facet acts as a window to the self (the consciousness or soul). It also acts as a mirror to promote recapitulation and self-reflection. To access this information through meditation, hold the diamond-shaped facet to the Third Eye Chakra. These crystals can help you to discover your soul path.

Starting the Journey

We all need to set aside time for our own personal healing and connection with crystals. It is my mission with this book to inspire you to do exactly that! Use the FREE BONUS resources that I have included on the next few pages to help get you acquainted with crystals.

For me, meditation is a common way to connect with my crystals and use them for healing and rejuvenation. Meditation is different for everyone, but there are a few key steps that can help to ensure that you have a great meditative experience.

1. Make yourself comfortable.
2. Release any expectations you may have about what you "should" feel, experience, etc. during the meditation.
3. Cleanse your crystals and your sacred space before beginning the session and after you have finished.
4. Don't get frustrated if you realize your mind has been wandering - just take a deep, centering breath , let it go, and get back in the moment.

What are you waiting for? It's time to jump right in! Take the next step toward enhancing your connection with crystals by downloading these helpful, FREE BONUS tools.

GET YOUR BONUS CRYSTAL JOURNEY MEDITATION mp3!

Just for reading this book and taking the first steps on your crystal journey, I want to give you a free gift...our "Crystal Journey Meditation" guided meditation mp3 audio file!

Go to http://tinyurl.com/crystaljourneymeditation to get your FREE BONUS meditation now!

Crystal Journey Meditation Notes

Date: _____

Type of Crystal Used: _____

Draw a picture of your crystal (or paste one below):

What was most noticeable about the physical appearance of your crystal when you visualized it in your mind's eye?

_____
_____
_____
_____

Discuss any guidance or any inner knowing you received about how this crystal can be used for healing:

_____
_____
_____
_____
_____

Another <u>FREE BONUS</u> for You!

To help start you on your crystal journey, I want to give you access to a downloadable, printable version of the "Crystal Journey Meditation Notes"! I hope they serves you well while you explore the mineral kingdom.

Go to http://tinyurl.com/crystaljourneynotes to get your FREE BONUS journal pages!

Another **FREE BONUS** for You!

Check out this helpful video for a more visual meditation experience! A guided visual journey, this video will help to connect with your crystals and with your spirit guides!

Go to http://tinyurl.com/ crystalmeditationvideo to watch your FREE BONUS video now!

Crystalline Blessings

"Every particular in nature, a leaf, a drop, a crystal, a moment of time is related to the whole, and partakes of the perfection of the whole." -Ralph Waldo Emerson

I leave you now to start your crystal journey, but I hope that you continue to use this book as a guide and reference to the many unique members of the mineral kingdom.

"The journey of a thousand miles begins with one step." -Lao Tzu

Crystal blessings always and in all ways,

Ashley Leavy

Founder & Educational Director of the
Love & Light School of Energy Medicine
www.LoveAndLightHealingSchool.com

Glossary of Terms

Akashic Records - This is thought to be the etheric version of collective history, accessible by those who have the necessary skills or tools, in order to gather information about your lifetimes, soul path, human history and future, and the planetary and universal influence on same. It is said by many to be a record of everything that has been and will be.

All That Is - The energy that connects and permeates all things in the Universe. A term used to describe everything that exists, both known and unknown.

Angels - These are beings of light that act as the messengers of the Universe, facilitating the connection between humans and source energy. Angels help you with your day to day life; your Guardian Angel belongs to this group and works closely with you at all times.

Archangels - These are ascended Angels who are each attributed with special qualities or abilities. It is commonly thought that there are seven main Archangels: Michael, Gabriel, Raphael, Chamuel, Jophiel, Uriel, and Zadkiel.

Ascended Masters - A group of ascended beings thought to offer guidance and wisdom for living to the human race. Often regarded as personal guides, these masters are approached for information, healing, prayers, and more.

Ascension - This is the process of raising your energy frequency or rate of vibration (i.e. ascending from this realm to higher realms). It is often accompanied by ascension symptoms.

Ascension Symptoms - A variety of physical symptoms, many of which can be quite uncomfortable or strange, that seem to accompany the ascension process. It is thought that as the physical body's energy vibration is lifted into the more etheric realms, the body must go through equivalent energetic changes as it evolves or ascends. This shift from the physical frequency toward the ethereal frequency results in these symptoms for the time that the body is adjusting to the new vibratory rate.

Astral Travel - This is the act of journeying to other realms or dimensions throughout space and time using the astral (or ethereal) body rather than the physical body.

Aura - This is the energy field that surrounds a sentient being. It is often viewed as consisting of many layers, each corresponding to a different part of that being (i.e. physical, emotional, mental, spiritual, etc.).

Centering - This is the process of becoming focused on the present moment.

Chakra - Chakras are vortices of energy found in the aura, or energy field, of the human body. These energy centers act as satellites to the universe, taking in energy, using it to influence the mind, the body, and the spirit, and then returning it back to the universe.

Each chakra rules a specific section of the physical body, a certain set of emotions, and specific aspects of your spiritual self. There are seven major chakras found along the spine, but there are many other minor chakras located throughout the entire physical body.

Charging - The process of infusing an object with energy.

Cleansing - This is the process of removing negative or unnecessary/unwanted energy from an object or environment, and transforming that energy into positivity for the highest good of all beings.

Crystal - This refers to any mineral with a regularly-repeating, internal, atomic structure (a crystalline lattice) that is formed from building-block-like units of matter. The physical appearance of the crystal (including it facets, sides, etc.) reflect this internal arrangement of molecules.

Ethereal - This term refers to the energetic portion of a sentient being (rather than to the physical), but can also denote a higher vibrational realm or dimension than that in which we live.

Etheric - Please see Ethereal

Face - Also known as a facet, this is one of the flat, exterior surfaces that helps to form the termination (or point) of the crystal.

Facet - Please see Face

Grid - This is a group of crystals placed in a concise, geometric arrangement (usually in sacred space) in order to affect the flow of energy for a specific purpose or intention. Crystal are powerful on their own, but when placed together, with intention, in a sacred geometrical pattern, their energy increases exponentially, becoming much more powerful than just the sum of the individual parts (especially after activation). The combination of the crystal energy with sacred geometry (which is the language of the universe) clearly communicates the intention for the grid to the Universal Source, allowing for rapid and powerful shifts in the energy frequency of the space in which the grid is located.

Grounding - This is the process of connecting with the energy of the earth to provide you with stability, protection, and balance.

Higher Self - This is the part of you that is your perfect, whole, most authentic self.

Inclusion - Also known as an occlusion, this term refers to any mineral growth occurring within a crystal structure.

Inner Self - This is the part of you that is your innermost, subconscious self.

Layout - This is the procedure of placing healing crystals on and around a person's body in order to maintain the flow of energy, correct imbalances, repair leaks, and remove blockages in your energy field, or aura.

Lightworker - This is a person who has dedicated your life to promoting the evolution of consciousness on our planet. Lightworkers live their lives with compassion and always act for the highest good of all beings.

Meditation - This is is the act of focusing and concentrating your mental energy until you have reached a perfect stillness of mind.

Mineral Kingdom - This is the Kingdom (or group) that contains all of the Earth's crystals and stones.

Occlusion - Please see Inclusion

Pineal Gland - This is a small, conical, endocrine gland located within the brain; it is very important to the central nervous system. The pineal gland is related to the Third Eye Chakra and has been said to hold the secret to spiritual evolution. It is activated during meditation and guided visualizations.

Reiki - This is an energy healing technique in which the practitioner channels energy (via the use of visualized healing symbols) into the client's body and energy field, through a light physical touch, using specific hand positions, in order to return balance to the client's body.

Sacred Geometry - This is the idea that some geometric shapes are linked with spiritual concepts, and that they correspond to certain attributes or properties. Some geometric principles or patterns are reflected over and over in our physical world; these are thought to have special significance and energetic frequencies.

Sacred Space - This is your personal sanctuary. It is a space in which you are completely comfortable; it provides a place where you can connect to the Universal Source.

Spirit Guides - This may be one or more personal guides or teachers, found in the ethereal realm that may provide you with information or messages, healing, and more.

Totem Animal - This is a special Spirit Guide that appears in the form of an animal being. This animal may be one that already holds special significance for you, or it may present itself as an animal with which you have not had any prior connection. It is often seen as a symbol representing a person's inner nature or Inner Self.

Vibrational Frequency - This term describes the rate of vibration or frequency within an object. A lower vibration typically denotes a strong connection to earth energy whereas a higher vibration typically denotes a strong connection to ethereal energy.

Yin and Yang - This is an ancient Chinese concept of interdependent origination whereby all things that exist are dependent upon one another and give rise to one another. This concept shows that each person's consciousness is just one part of All That Is. It represents our dual existence (physical/spiritual, microcosm/macrocosm, body/mind, etc).

Index

Term	*Page #*

Akashic Record - 46-48, 50, 62, 67, 83, 109, 111, 113, 143, 149-150, 159

All That Is - 41, 151, 159, 164

Angel - 8, 16, 18, 20-21, 23, 28-29, 43-44, 53-54, 66-68, 71, 78, 82, 85-86, 90-91, 98-101, 104, 108-110, 112-113, 117, 119, 136, 139, 159

Ascended Master - 17, 90, 139, 159

Ascension - 11-12, 15, 17, 20, 23-24, 26, 29, 34, 37, 40, 47, 51, 67, 69, 73, 76, 78, 80, 82-83, 85, 88, 90-91, 96-97, 99-101, 103, 108-109, 111, 113, 117, 122-124, 141, 160

Astral Travel - 11, 18, 20, 24, 28-29, 49, 52, 54-55, 61, 63-64, 66-68, 70-73, 77, 82, 84, 87, 89, 93, 95-98, 100-102, 104-105, 109, 111, 113-114, 116-118, 123, 135, 160

Aura - 20, 22-23, 29-30, 35, 45, 50-52, 56, 64, 66, 72, 80, 86-90, 92-93, 95, 97-101, 104, 111, 113, 115, 160, 162

Centering - 7, 9, 79, 85, 153, 160

Chakra - 7, 133, 152, 160-161, 163

Cleansing - 17, 20, 22-234, 26-27, 29, 31, 33, 35-36, 39, 41-45, 51, 57, 59, 61, 64, 77, 89, 92, 100-101, 105, 109-111, 113, 117, 120, 153, 161

Crystal - 161

Ethereal - 38, 61, 64, 67-68, 70, 81, 83-84, 89, 93, 106, 119-120, 135, 159-161, 164

Face - 130, 133, 135, 137-138, 143, 146, 149-150, 152, 161

Grid - 7, 94, 105, 128, 137, 162

Grounding - 8-13, 16-18, 26-27, 30, 33, 38-39, 46-47, 49-50, 54-55, 58, 60, 62-63, 65, 69-72, 75-76, 78, 84, 89, 92, 95-96, 102, 104-106, 108, 110, 112, 118-121, 125-126, 137, 162

Higher Self - 16-17, 51, 69, 78, 90, 93, 109, 162

Inclusion - 10, 12, 20, 32, 42, 78, 85, 87-89, 91-92, 94, 101-102, 105, 107, 142, 162-163

Inner Self - 27, 33, 49, 53, 70, 83, 90-91, 140, 162, 164

Layout - 105, 162

Lightworker - 92, 94, 163

Meditation - 5, 12, 14-16, 18, 21-24, 28-29, 31, 34, 36, 40, 43-44, 46, 51-52, 59, 61, 63, 82, 85-86, 88, 90, 92-97, 99, 101-103, 105-106, 108, 111, 113-117, 120, 125, 130, 133, 135-136, 146, 152-157, 163

Mineral Kingdom - 5, 156, 158, 163

Pineal Gland - 74, 108, 163

Reiki - 20, 35, 76, 163

Sacred Geometry - 24, 69, 162-163

Sacred Space - 54, 153, 162, 164

Spirit Guide - 8, 10-11, 16, 21-22, 25, 28-29, 34, 42, 44, 46, 54, 59, 66-68, 71-72, 78, 82, 84-87, 90, 103, 109-110, 116-117, 126, 139, 157, 159, 164

Totem Animal - 8, 10-11, 16, 23, 34, 42, 44, 46, 49, 52, 54, 59-60, 66-68, 71, 82, 87, 90, 103, 110, 117, 125-127, 139, 164

Vibrational Frequency - 15-17, 28, 54, 60, 70, 80, 89, 96, 99-101, 124, 131, 160-161, 164

Yin and Yang - 36, 55, 75, 126, 164

More About Us

Create a Life & Sacred Business that are Aligned with *YOUR* Inner Beliefs!

> "If you follow your bliss, you put yourself on a kind of track that has been there all the while waiting for you."
> -Joseph Campbell

Follow Your Bliss!

We believe that everyone deserves the opportunity to be happy in their lives, sharing healing, and doing work that they love to do! Our programs embody our mission is to inspire, educate, and support Energy Healers and Lightworkers who are following their dreams and making a difference in the world through the work that they do and the service that they provide to others.

Sharing expert-tested healing techniques; creating a supportive, like-minded, heart-centered network of people, and showing healers and energy workers how to embrace a life aligned with their spiritual path is what our school is all about.

We want to inspire you to start living the life that you were always meant to live, by developing your healing skills and, more importantly, by helping you to create a life that you truly love.

Is Love & Light's Crystal Healing Certification Program right for *YOU*?

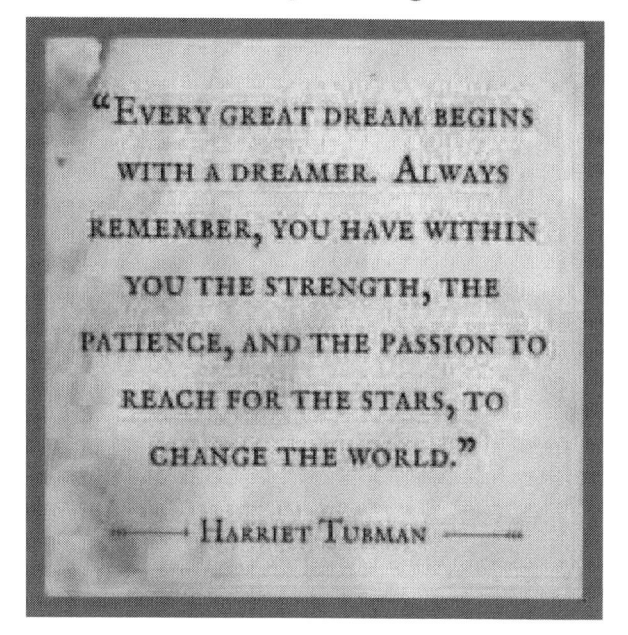

> "EVERY GREAT DREAM BEGINS WITH A DREAMER. ALWAYS REMEMBER, YOU HAVE WITHIN YOU THE STRENGTH, THE PATIENCE, AND THE PASSION TO REACH FOR THE STARS, TO CHANGE THE WORLD."
>
> — HARRIET TUBMAN

Follow Your Heart to a Life & Career You LOVE

Follow your heart and let it be the compass on your life's journey; if you follow your heart, then the universe will support you. One person is all it takes to create a positive force for change. Integrating energy healing into your life and your sacred business *WILL* support the positive change of our planet. You have something special and sacred that is unique to you. You have a gift - share it with the world! Take the next step to sharing your gift and creating positive change by enrolling in our Crystal Healing Certification Program.

- Are you ready to take the first step toward big changes in your life?
- Are you ready to make a difference in the lives of others & be a force for positive change?
- Are you ready to start a ripple effect that will send healing energy out into the universe?

Why You Should Become a Certified Crystal Healer (CCH):

Our Crystal Healing Certification Program provides a practical, comprehensive crystal therapy education. The classes in this program help heart-centered, dedicated learners to build thriving crystal healing practices. By completing this program, you will learn to have a career and life that you love, all while developing new skills that will allow you to benefit your family, your friends, your clients, and yourself. Working with your natural gifts and developing your healing skills will help you to be of service to yourself and others, creating positive energy and working toward personal and planetary healing.

No matter what the reason, you will be developing skills and learning techniques that you can apply to all areas of your life - growing as you go. Education is one of the best ways to hone your skills, so that you can continue to shine your light into the world.

This program will provide a foundation for your journey into the world of Crystal Healing, supporting you on your path and guiding you toward a deep connection and understanding of the crystal realm (while helping to develop your healing skills and making you more marketable and successful in YOUR sacred business).

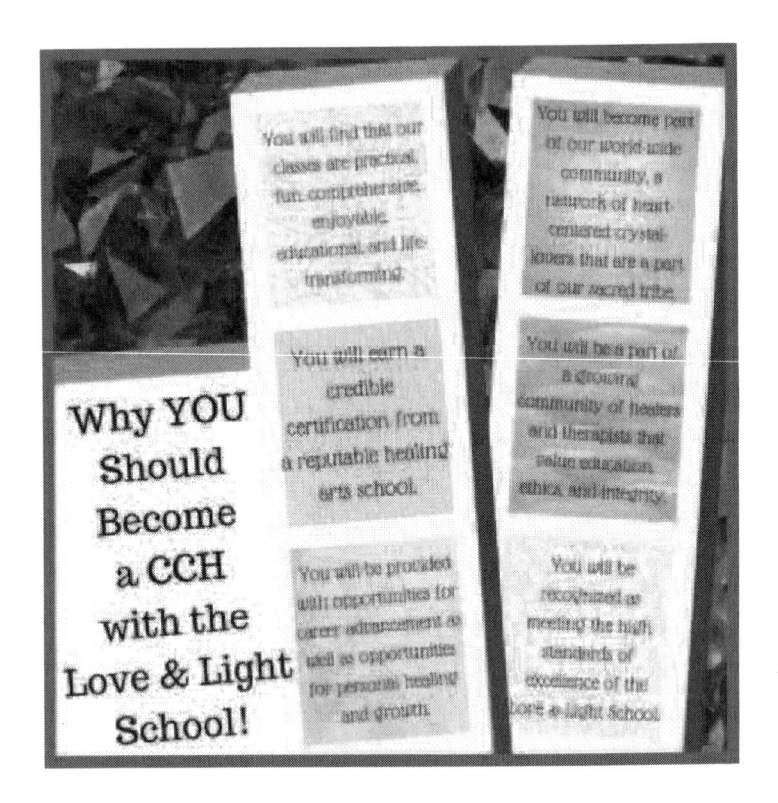

Why YOU Should Become a CCH with the Love & Light School!

- You will find that our classes are practical, fun, comprehensive, enjoyable, educational, and life-transforming.
- You will become part of our world-wide community, a network of heart-centered crystal-lovers that are a part of our sacred tribe.
- You will earn a credible certification from a reputable healing arts school.
- You will be a part of a growing community of healers and therapists that value education, ethics, and integrity.
- You will be provided with opportunities for career advancement as well as opportunities for personal healing and growth.
- You will be recognized as meeting the high standards of excellence of the Love & Light School.

Ready to Find Your Passion & Purpose?

We know that with the right knowledge, you will have the tools to create a life you love.

It is important to us to see you succeed because we believe that everyone deserves to live a happy life, following their life path while being financially and spiritually supported and fulfilled. We provide compassionate crystal-lovers and energy healing enthusiasts with expert training and knowledge.

Our classes and programs will provide you with professional, high-quality, energy healing education and training so that you can:

- be of service to others and help those in need with YOUR unique gifts
- build and transition into a successful, alternative career
- share your unique gifts with the world
- become a part of an amazing network of heart-centered healers and entrepreneurs
- learn the "hows" and "whys" of crystal healing along with step-by-step instructions on how to perform a variety of crystal healing techniques (specific to each class topic)
- gain clarity and learn to be more confident when giving crystal healing sessions professionally
- grow both spiritually and emotionally
- learn the "best practices" for maintaining ethics and integrity in your healing practice and sacred business
- become professionally certified by a reputable school (which helps make your sacred business more credible)
- enhance your potential for career advancement and increased income (because clients and employers will value the knowledge and diverse skills you learn in the program)
- utilize skills for your own self-healing and care (because these are essential for personal and business growth; when you're happy and healthy, your clients will be too!)

Because our school has set a standard of excellence in the energy healing community, your clients will have peace of mind knowing that you were trained at a reputable energy healing school that provides professional, quality education.

By enrolling in one of our certification programs, you are taking the next step toward working with natural healing energy every day (whether professionally to enhance your career, personally to work through your own self-healing, or so that you may answer your calling to be of service to friends and family members in need of healing).

Take the first step on your journey to more prosperity, new opportunities, and spiritual fulfillment! You can learn to create a life and a sacred business that you love by enrolling in our Crystal Healing Certification Program!

Are you READY to say *YES* to an exciting new journey?

Our Crystal Healing Certification Program, taught by Ashley Leavy, can be completed online through a simple, convenient, virtual classroom (either in a live, scheduled class or via a pre-recorded class video that can be accessed at any time).

The online classes are very simple to use. You will receive a manual and a pre-recorded training video for each class in the program (11 in total).

After reading the manual and watching the recording of the class video, you will take a multiple choice exam (online). After you successfully complete all 11 exams, you have completed the program.

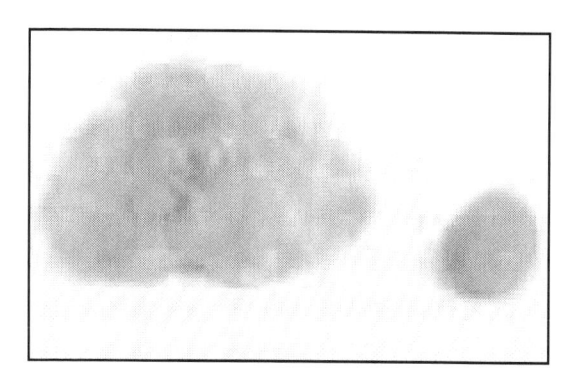

You have 2 certification options, you may choose to receive 1 certificate for each individual class (totaling 11 certificates), or you may wait until the end of the program and receive 1 certificate for the whole thing. No matter which option you choose, you will earn 26 continuing education hours through NCBTMB and you will be recognized as a CCH.

Why choose the Love & Light School?

The classes are organized and guided so that you can focus on the content (and not be confused by how things are organized or what you're supposed to do next).

The on-demand format is great for people with busy or inflexible schedules which allows students to take classes on their own time (regardless of schedule conflicts, time zone differences, unexpected events, etc.). This allows our students to take their time and absorb information rather than being rushed by a deadline (we do not have time limits for class completion), but it also provides an option for students who would like to fast-track their education. We have had some students finish this 11-part Crystal Healing Certification Program in as little as two weeks.

The distance-learning format makes it possible for people who do not have access to a healing arts school in their area to get a top-quality crystal healing education.

One-on-one instructor email guidance and email technical support are included. This guarantees that each student will receive one-on-one interaction with the instructor (via email) even though the included classes are pre-recorded.

Alumni of this program will receive a special listing on the Alumni Page of our website, which provides our graduates with free marketing and publicity as well as creating a positive affiliation with our reputable healing arts school.

Build a strong foundation for success with our Crystal Healing Certification Program!

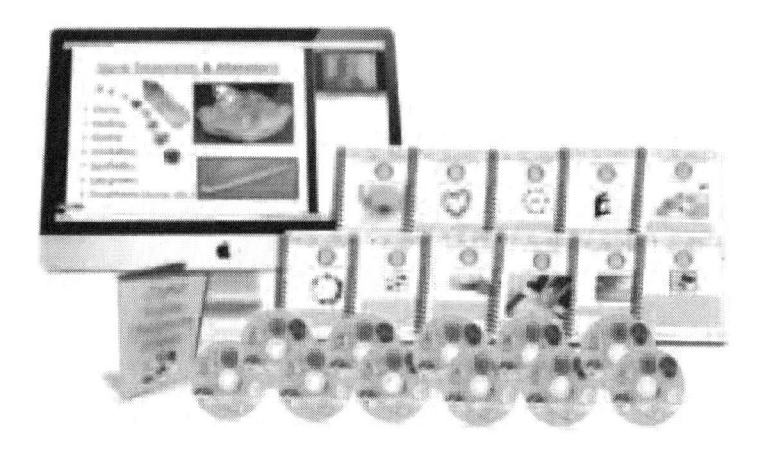

What is Included with this Program?

- 11 webinar style classes (listed above) including instructor video and a slideshow presentation
- 11 comprehensive PDF class manuals (accessible through our virtual classroom)
- Instructor email support
- Unlimited technical support
- Lifetime access to class materials and updates
- BONUS class resources (videos, articles, mp3s, & more)

Program Class Listing:
1) Basic Crystal Healing
2) Sensing Subtle Energy with Stones & Crystals
3) Advanced Crystal Healing
4) Energetic Protection with Crystals & Stones
5) Basic Crystal Healing Layouts
6) Advanced Crystal Healing Layouts
7) Chakra Healing with Crystals & Stones
8) Working with Crystal Grids
9) Emotional Healing with Crystals
10) Using Crystals for Fertility Treatment
11) Creating a Crystal Healing Mandala

Are you ready to TRANSFORM your life and your sacred business?

What Happens When I Complete the Program?

- You will be a Certified Crystal Healer through the Love & Light School of Energy Medicine and will be able to use the letters "CCH" after your name.
- You will have earned 26 Continuing Education Hours (approved by NCBTMB).
- Your Certification as a CCH will identify you as having received comprehensive, quality, crystal healing education and training from a reputable source.
- You will get to CELEBRATE your great accomplishment!!!

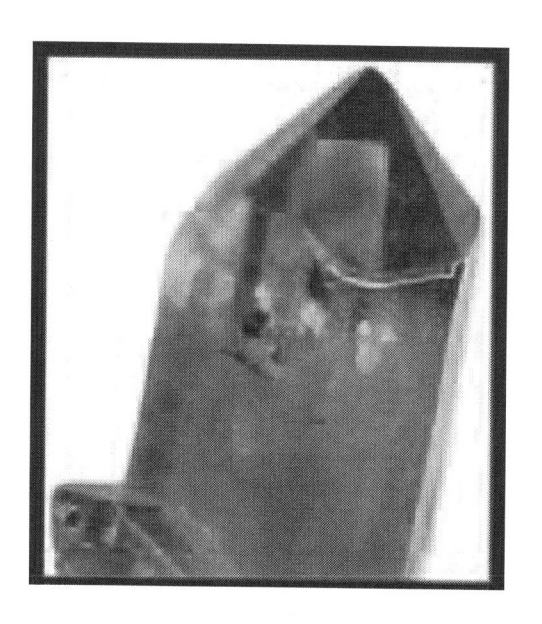

Enroll in our Crystal Healing Certification Program and Learn to Create the Career of Your Dreams!

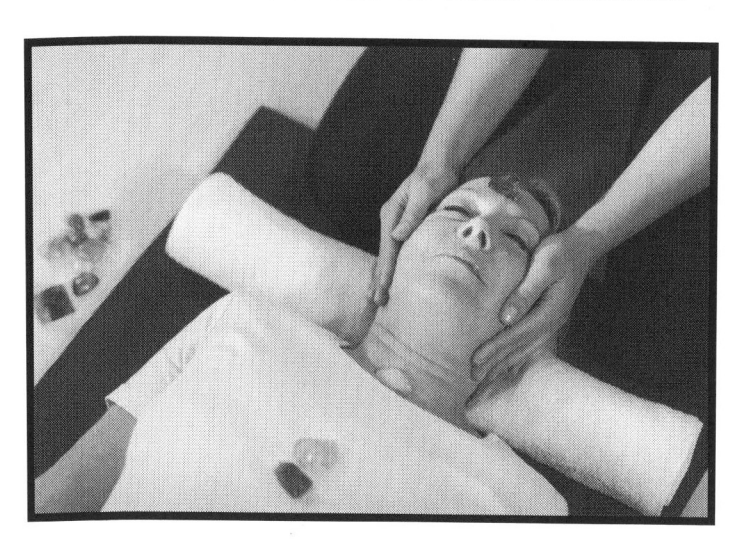

Made in the USA
Lexington, KY
04 April 2019